Shark Attack!

Gail
Tuchman

SCHOLASTIC INC.

New York   Toronto   London   Auckland
Sydney   Mexico City   New Delhi   Hong Kong

Read more! Do more!

Download your free all-new digital book,
Shark Attack! Reading Fun

Quizzes to test your knowledge and reading skills

Fun activities to share what you've discovered

Log on to
www.scholastic.com/discovermore/readers
Enter this special code: L2DMFXD77452

Contents

EDUCATIONAL BOARD:
Monique Datta, EdD, Asst. Professor, Rossier School of Education, USC;
Karyn Saxon, PhD, Elementary Curriculum Coordinator, Wayland, MA;
Francie Alexander, Chief Academic Officer, Scholastic Inc.

Distributed in the UK by Scholastic UK Ltd, Westfiel   utham,
Warwickshire, England CV47 0R

ISBN 978-1-407-13835-0

10 9 8 7 6 5 4 3 2 1   13 14 1

Printed in the USA   40
First published 2013

KT-162-534

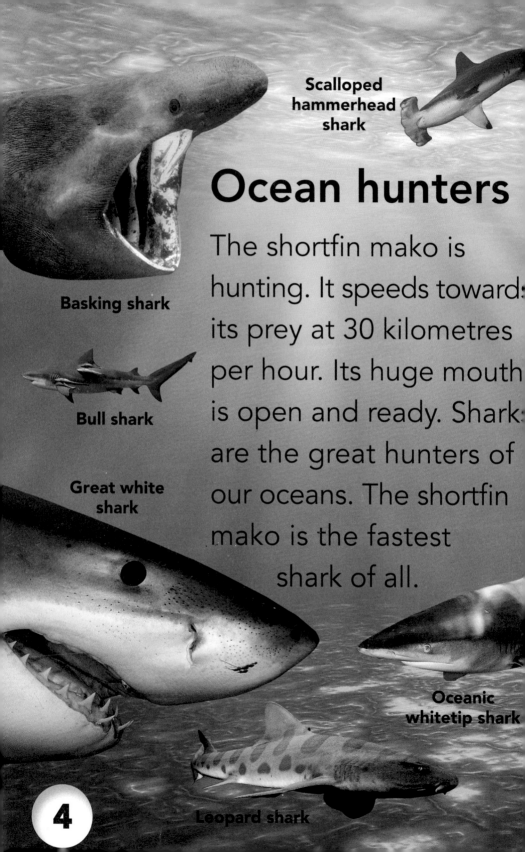

Scalloped hammerhead shark

Ocean hunters

The shortfin mako is hunting. It speeds towards its prey at 30 kilometres per hour. Its huge mouth is open and ready. Sharks are the great hunters of our oceans. The shortfin mako is the fastest shark of all.

Basking shark

Bull shark

Great white shark

Oceanic whitetip shark

Leopard shark

Tiger shark

NEW WORD

prey

pray

An animal that is **prey** is hunted down and may be killed by another animal.

SAY IT OUT LOUD

Caribbean reef sharks

Silky shark

Shortfin mako shark

Here are more supercool sharks. Sharks are fish. The whale shark is the biggest shark. It's the world's biggest fish. It can grow to 12 metres long.

How big am I?   Dwarf lanternshark   Human

The 18-cm dwarf lanternshark fits into a person's hand. Its belly glows. It can't be seen from below. This hides the shark from animals that want to eat it!

This is the smallest shark in the ocean.

This is the biggest shark in the ocean.

Whale shark

T. rex

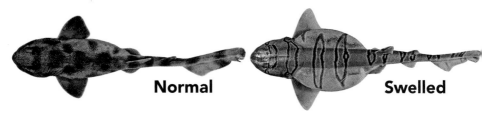

Normal **Swelled**

The swell shark has a secret.
It can swallow lots of water and
swell up to twice its size. Now it's
hard for another animal to bite it.

The shortfin mako can leap
6 metres out of the water!

420 million years ago

Sharks are living
in the ocean.

200 mya

Dinosaurs rule
the planet.

Sharks are survivors. They've been swimming in our waters for more than 400 million years. Sharks were here long before *T. rex* and humans were!

Ancient sharks ate dinosaurs that fell into the sea!

60 mya

Mammals thrive.

190,000 years ago

Humans are living in Africa.

Amazing bodies

Why have sharks survived so long?
Their amazing bodies make them
the best hunters in the ocean.
A shark's skeleton is made
of cartilage. Cartilage bends
more easily than bone
does. It helps the
shark twist and turn
in the water.

**Great white
shark**

It's a
fact!

A shark takes in
water to breathe.
The water leaves
the body through
the gill slits.

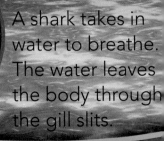

Sharks never run out of teeth.

Fins help a shark move forward, balance, and steer.

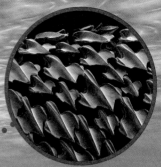

Denticles are rough scales that protect a shark's body.

Teeth are the bony parts of a shark. A shark can use 30,000 teeth in its life.

If a tooth falls out, a new one moves in.

You have five senses.
Sharks have six super senses
to track down their prey.

Hearing Sharks hear
sounds too low for
you to hear.

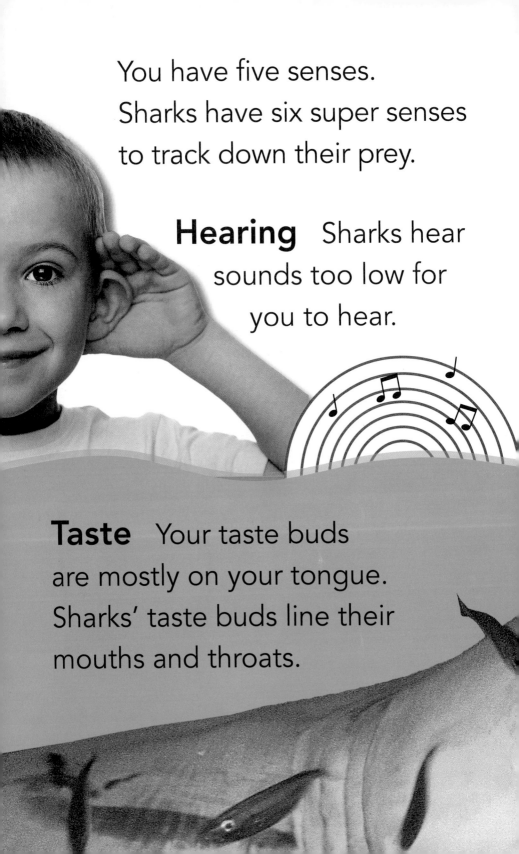

Taste Your taste buds
are mostly on your tongue.
Sharks' taste buds line their
mouths and throats.

Some sharks can smell blood up to 5 kilometres away.

Nurse shark

Smell You use your nose to smell and breathe. Sharks use theirs for smelling prey.

A great white takes a test bite. It tastes to find out if its prey is good to eat.

13

Sight Sharks can see about ten times better in low light than you can.

The blue shark has a special layer in its eye for seeing in the dark sea.

Touch You feel things when you touch them. Sharks feel vibrations from things *before* they touch them.

Electroreception Sharks have a sixth sense. They sense electricity in other animals. This helps them find out where dinner is hiding!

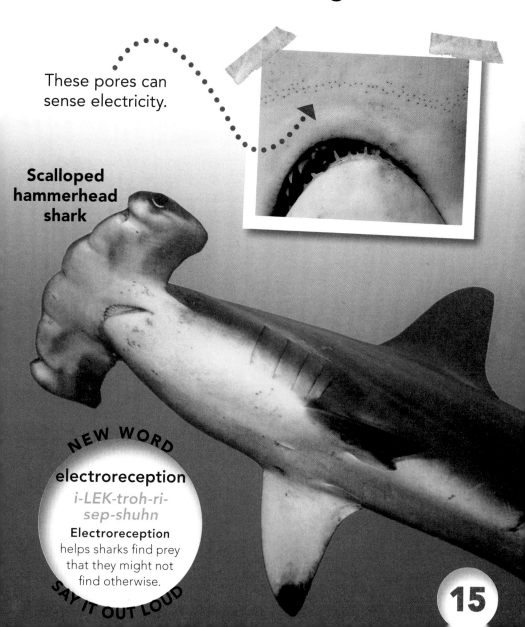

These pores can sense electricity.

Scalloped hammerhead shark

Eat up!

A shark's main job is feeding. Sharks rarely attack humans to eat them. People are bony and don't taste good. Sharks eat fish and other smaller ocean animals. They even eat other sharks!

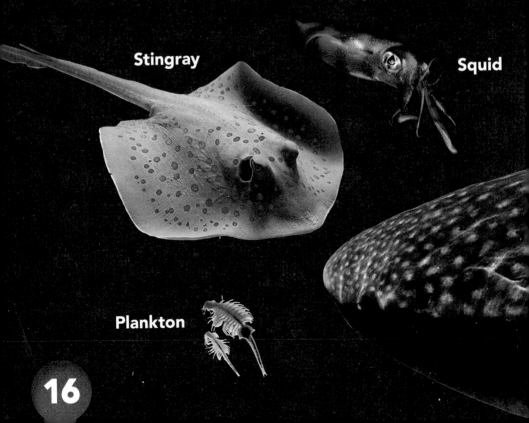

Old boot

Stingray

Squid

Plankton

A tiger shark
will eat anything –
even a boot!

The nurse shark traps
and sucks up squid.

The hammerhead
shark likes stingrays
best of all.

The giant whale shark
eats tiny plankton –
tonnes of it!

A great
white shark
tracks a seal.
The seal is rich
in fat. The shark
swims fast, near the
top of the water. It's now
a few metres from the seal.
The great white points its
snout upwards. It bursts out
of the water with its jaws open
wide. It pushes its upper jaw and
teeth forwards. Its teeth find their
mark. *Chomp!*

It's a fact!

After eating a baby seal, a great white

can survive 12–15 days without feeding.

A horn shark scents an egg case. It bites with strong jaws and flat back teeth – *crunch!*

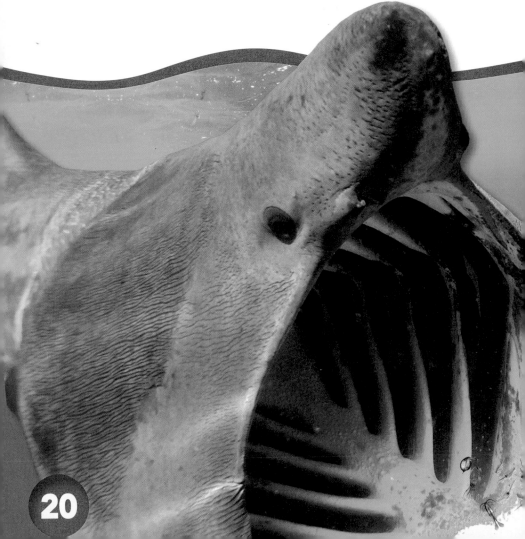

Slurp! A cookie-cutter shark attaches its lips to prey. It bites using pointy, razor-sharp teeth. The shark cuts out a bite as round as a cookie!

A basking shark glides through the sea. Its mouth is open. It collects water, and strains out plankton with its gill rakers.

NEW WORD

plankton
PLANGK-tuhn
Tiny animals drifting in the ocean are **plankton**.

SAY IT OUT LOUD

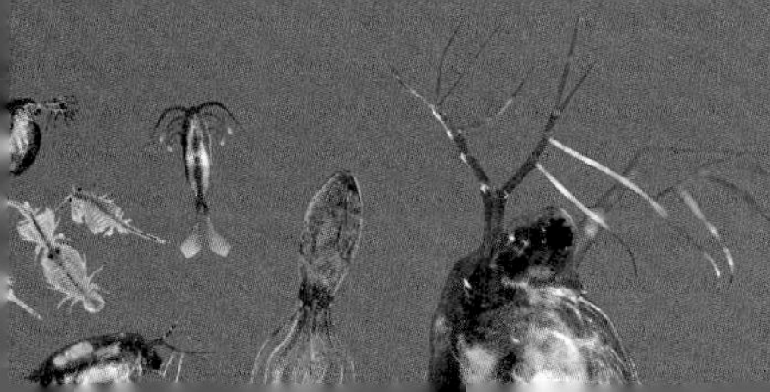

21

Coral reefs teem with ocean life. One in four kinds of all ocean animals are found here.

Whitetip reef shark

Coral reefs are made from the skeletons of billions of tiny sea creatures.

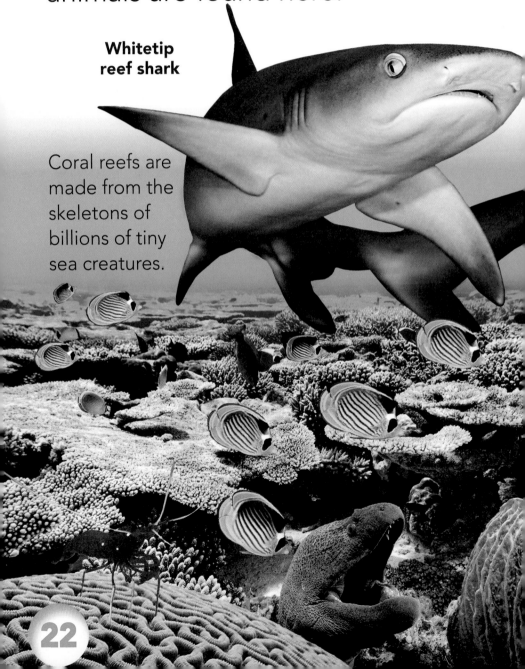

Sharks rule coral reefs. They keep reefs healthy by eating weak and sick animals.

Blacktip reef shark

Shark attacks

People are more likely to be killed by sharks in Australia than in any other place. But the number of attacks is small.

5

3

COCOS
ISLANDS

AUSTRALIA

WESTERN
AUSTRALIA

65

Around the world, crocodiles, dogs, and pigs each kill more people every year than sharks do. People are a much bigger danger to sharks than sharks are to people.

This map shows the number of shark attacks in Australia between 1700 and 2012. The total is **510.**

NORTHERN TERRITORY

161

QUEENSLAND

SOUTH AUSTRALIA

NEW SOUTH WALES

35

195

VICTORIA

33

13

TASMANIA

Sharks under attack

Humans are sharks' main predators. As many as 100 million sharks are killed by people every year.

Shark fins are used to make shark fin soup.

Many sharks are caught in nets set for other fish.

Dr Ellen K. Pikitch is a scientist and "shark hugger". She says:

"Sharks are sensitive creatures. They need our help. They must not be killed in the numbers they are now. One way to help them is to create safe areas where they won't be hunted. We must work to get the word out about the dangers sharks face."

World of sharks

We humans find sharks to be both terrifying and beautiful. There are more than 400 kinds of sharks in our seas. They are unlike any other animals on Earth. Let's help

Blue sharks feed on a school of anchovies in the warm waters off California, USA.

them survive. Let's keep the seas swimming with supercool sharks. Their future depends on our respect for them and their watery world.

Glossary

anchovy
A small ocean fish that may be salted and canned for people to eat.

cartilage
A strong, flexible material that forms a shark's skeleton.

denticle
A rough scale that helps protect a shark's body.

electroreception
The sense system that sharks use to detect electric signals given off by other animals.

fin
A stiff part on a shark that moves it forward through the water or helps it balance or steer.

gill raker
A body part in certain sharks that catches and strains food from the water.

gill slit
An opening on a fish's body out of which water passes after the fish has used it to breathe.

plankton
Tiny animals and plants that drift or float in oceans or lakes.

predator
An animal that hunts other animals for food.

prey
An animal that is hunted by another animal for food.

reef
A strip of rock, sand, or coral just below the surface of a body of water.

scale
A thin, flat piece of hard skin on a fish's body.

sensitive
Affected even by very small changes.

skeleton
The set of bones that supports and protects the bodies of some animals.

steer
To make something go in a particular direction.

survivor
Someone or something that lives for a long time or through hard times.

swallow
To make food or drink move from the mouth to the stomach.

teem
To be very full of.

thrive
To be healthy and strong.

vibration
A fast movement back and forth.

Index

Image credits

Photography and artwork
1: Andy Murch/Visuals Unlimited; 2cl: Andreas Meyer/Shutterstock; 2–3b (water): Irochka/Fotolia; 3: Rob Stegmann/iStockphoto; 4–5 (background): Nastco/iStockphoto; 4tl: Andy Murch/Visuals Unlimited; 4tc: Chris Dascher/iStockphoto; 4cl: Fiona Ayerst/iStockphoto; 4bl: Chris Dascher/iStockphoto; 4br: Reinhard Dirscherl/Visuals Unlimited; 4bc, 5l: Andy Murch/Visuals Unlimited; 5tc: Amanda Cotton/iStockphoto; 5crt, 5crm: Chris Dascher/iStockphoto; 5crb: Kadri Ates Evirgen/iStockphoto; 6–7 (main image): Alexis Rosenfeld/Science Photo Library/Science Source; 6 (human icon): Tulay Over/iStockphoto; 6–7 (whale shark icon): Scholastic Inc.; 7 (hand): peshkova/Fotolia; 7 (lanternshark): Seapics.com; 7 (dinosaur icon): Pro Web Design/Fotolia; 8t: T. Carter/Science Image/CSIRO; 8c: Mandy Hague; 9: Jon Hughes, jfhdigital.com; 10–11 (main image): Michael Patrick O'Neill/Science Source; 10bl: NatalyArt/Fotolia; 10bc: Alexis Rosenfeld/Science Photo Library/Science Source; 11tl: iLexx/iStockphoto; 11tr: Eye of Science/Science Source; 11br: BW Folsom/Shutterstock; 12cl: ia_64/Fotolia; 12cr: Scholastic Inc.; 12–13b: Mark Conlin/Alamy Images; 13 (blood): stockcam/iStockphoto; 13tr: Stephen Frink/Corbis Images; 14t: Masa Ushioda/Media Bakery; 14cr: gosphotodesign/Fotolia; 14b: Scholastic Inc.; 15cr: Doug Perrine/Nature Picture Library; 15b: iStockphoto/Thinkstock; 16 (t to b): Julian Rovagnati/Shutterstock, Cor Bosman/iStockphoto, bernd.neeser/Shutterstock, bluehand/Shutterstock; 17 (t to b): Albert kok/Wikipedia, Stephen Frink/Corbis Images, Seapics.com, Martin Strmiska/Alamy Images; 18–19 (t, b): Scholastic Inc.; 18–19 (main image): Fabrice Bettex/Alamy Images; 20tl: Marine Themes; 20b: Dan Burton/Nature Picture Library; 20–21b (various plankton): bluehand/Shutterstock, micro_photo/iStockphoto, digitalbalance/Fotolia; 21tr: Seapics.com; 21b: Louise Murray/Science Source; 22–23 (background): Tobias Helbig/iStockphoto; 22 (shark): David Fleetham/Visuals Unlimited; 22 (yellow fish): Richard Carey/iStockphoto; 22 (coral bl): microgen/iStockphoto; 22 (shrimp): rep0rter/iStockphoto; 22 (eel): Richard Carey/iStockphoto; 22–23 (coral bc): Dirk-Jan Mattaar/iStockphoto; 23 (sharks): R. Gino Santa Maria/Shutterstock; 23 (turtle): Zoonar/Thinkstock; 23 (yellow fish): Predrag Vuckovic/iStockphoto; 23 (clownfish br): marrio31/iStockphoto; 24–25 (background): iLexx/iStockphoto; 24–25 (map): Arunas Gabalis/Shutterstock; 24cl: Chris Dascher/iStockphoto; 25cr: Andreas Meyer/Shutterstock; 25br: Michael Patrick O'Neill/Science Source; 26–27t (blood): Scholastic Inc.; 26–27 (main image): Brian Skerry/National Geographic/Getty Images; 26 (bowl): studyoritim/iStockphoto; 26 (spoon): Scholastic Inc.; 27 (paper): Electric_Crayon/iStockphoto; 27 (tape): spxChrome/iStockphoto; 27 (photo frame): kevin llewellyn/iStockphoto; 27 (diver with shark): Institute for Ocean Conservation Science/Stony Brook University; 28–29: Seapics.com; 30–31: Chris Fallows/www.apexpredators.com.

Cover
Front cover: (icon) Jan Dabrowski/iStockphoto; (main image) Alexander Safonov/Getty Images; (bc) cameilia/Shutterstock; (br) Katseyephoto/Dreamstime. Back cover: (computer monitor) Manaemedia/Dreamstime. Inside front cover: (all) Scholastic Inc.

Thank you
For their generosity of time in sharing their expertise, special thanks to: George H. Burgess, Director of the Florida Program for Shark Research and Curator of the International Shark Attack File, Florida Museum of Natural History; Dr. Ellen K. Pikitch, marine biologist and Executive Director of the Institute for Ocean Conservation Science, Stony Brook University School of Marine and Atmospheric Sciences; Drury Thorp, cofounder of Shark Savers; Kim Dennis-Bryan, for expert consultation; and Mike Coots, for sharing his passion. Shark attack data on pages 24–25 © International Shark Attack File, Florida Museum of Natural History, University of Florida.

CONTENTS

FOREWORD

Many companies are coming to grips with the reality of managing their European brands and business. Our own company, Lever, has been strongly established in Europe for most of a century. But the developments that have led to the creation of a single European market, and the recognition in our industry that we were engaged in playing in a European game, has led us to evolve new organizations and management structures in order, quickly and decisively, to exploit the opportunities presented.

Innovation, quality and speed of implementation are crucial issues to overall business success. We have worked hard to find a blend of central control and national sensitivity, a mix of global strategy with strongly based national operations, which will work well for Lever in Europe.

This issue becomes particularly tricky in the case of sales promotion activities. Large sums of money are spent on sales promotion by many multinationals working in Europe. However, the complexities involved in many promotions have so far made many companies shy away from trying to co-ordinate this area of their marketing on a European basis. As everywhere, there are advantages in cohesion, speed, economies of scale, from recognizing the wider opportunity.

The example of Coca-Cola, Burger King and Ghostbusters – page 166 of this book – is a sign of the way ahead, but it is still something of a *rara avis*. There will be many more to come.

Alan Toop is uniquely well qualified to write on this subject, having spent many years working in the field, over a period where he has been able to create, assess and manage promotion on a national, as well as a European, basis. Through 20 years of consultancy with a range of leading companies in Europe, Alan is now able to write what is a pioneering work on the subject of European promotions.

It will be read with interest by business managers, like myself, who need all the help and insights that they can get to manage their way ahead in what is an increasingly complex and fast-moving European business world.

Written with quiet good humour and well-informed objectivity, the book itself is a pleasure to read. It is a carefully structured blend of basic business philosophies and approaches, with frequent and widely derived insights and perceptions about the scope, and the limitations, of sales promotion techniques. The range of cases covered is wide and illuminating. There is something for everybody here.

This is a distinguished addition to the still small body of authoritative literature on sales promotion, and to the growing body of work which can help the business manager to plot the course forward in European management.

I recommend it warmly to everyone who has any involvement with sales promotion.

Andrew Seth
Chief Executive
Lever Brothers Ltd, UK

ACKNOWLEDGEMENTS

My thanks go to all the companies whose promotions are featured in the following pages and to their agencies whose work is acknowledged in each case study.

The following individuals have been especially helpful in tracking down and obtaining material for this book: Iain Arthur; Jacques Bourgoin; Maurice Cohen; Carmela Ficara; Peter Freiss; Aude de Heurtaumont-Toulin; Jill Lewis; Sue Short; Enzo Torre; Alain Willard.

Karen May has kindly contributed the Footnote on Eastern Europe and the Commonwealth of Independent States in Appendix A.

Any mistakes are my own.

1

INTRODUCTION

THE BOOM IN SALES PROMOTION

The past quarter of a century has seen a tremendous boom in sales promotion activity across Europe. Sales promotion ranks high in any European league table of growth industries.

It's a boom which has taken a wide variety of forms, impacting on more and more areas of branding, marketing and selling, challenging many of our traditional assumptions about how products and services are best launched, distributed and made to appeal to their target users over time. This has led to a constant evolution in how companies structure their internal organizations, and what external services they employ.

Here are some of the key features of this boom.

EXPENDITURE

The money spent on sales promotion has been increasing year by year. For many brands in many companies in a growing number of European countries, the proportion of marketing support budgets spent on all forms of sales promotion equals or even exceeds the proportion spent on classic media advertising.

Even some of this media advertising is devoted to communicating messages about sales promotional offers, rather than messages about the brands themselves, their inherent benefits and competitive advantages.

The recent growth of direct marketing activities in certain countries has, in turn, fuelled sales promotion expenditure. For example, direct mail messages commonly include a promotional offer to encourage recipients to 'act now'.

BUSINESS SECTORS

Sales promotion techniques have been employed in an ever-increasing variety of industrial and commercial sectors. Twenty-five years ago most sales promotions were in support of fast moving consumer goods (fmcg): toiletries; soaps and detergents; packaged foods; petrol and oil; beers, wines and spirits; and tobacco (where legislation permitted) etc. Today we see almost every sector of business and commerce using sales promotions to help achieve their objectives: consumer durables such as cars, household appliances, and furniture and furnishing; clothing; airlines, railways and other transportation services; hotels and tour operators; personal financial services such as banking and insurance; broadcasting and other media; even housing and property; and government services.

The following chapters contain a number of case studies drawn from these 'newer' sectors for sales promotion.

PEOPLE

Hand in hand with this growth in activity has been an exponential growth in the number of people concerned full-time or part-time with sales promotion.

A range of specialist service companies now exists to source premiums and prizes; to handle mail or telephone applications for promotional offers; to distribute coupons and to clear their redemption; to mount special displays of promoted products and services in retail outlets; to print game cards under security conditions; to research the competitive appeal of alternative offers. Sales promotion agencies and consultancies dedicated to creating promotional concepts have emerged as an influential force.

Within the companies which own the brands, the scale of spending on sales promotion has required increasingly senior managers to concern themselves with this aspect of marketing. It is rarely adequate today to leave responsibility only in the hands of a specialist sales promotion manager, or alternatively to regard sales promotion as a useful activity for junior marketing personnel to 'cut their teeth on', while the marketing director concerns him or herself with 'more important' branding areas such as advertising and pack design – a not uncommon practice 25 years ago.

SKILLS AND EXPERTISE

Understanding of how best to use sales promotion techniques has become more widely diffused throughout marketing organisations, in line with this growth in expenditure. A whole generation of marketing personnel, brought up in a business environment in which sales promotion has been an important element in the marketing mix, has now reached the boardroom. This generation has learned much from this constant exposure to sales promotion, and has passed on these lessons to younger managers.

For newcomers to business, sales promotion is today taught and examined by many academic and professional institutions. And some well-informed literature on the subject now exists, though its volume is still very slim in relation to the crucial role that sales promotion now plays in the destinies of many brands. There are still 20 good books on advertising for every one on sales promotion.

IMPLICATIONS

The implications of these developments are fundamental to our understanding of brand marketing, to the extent that some brands now depend for their success or failure more on the skill with which they deploy sales promotional techniques than on any other marketing decisions.

WHY THIS BOOM?

There are many explanations for this boom – this apparently inexorable increase in sales promotional activity, year by year.

These are some of the key factors to consider.

COST-EFFECTIVENESS

This diffusion of understanding of how best to use sales promotion techniques has led to a realization that a wide variety of marketing objectives can, in some instances, be achieved most effectively and at lowest cost by these techniques; that is to say, by sales promotion techniques, rather than by other marketing tools such as advertising and public relations.

In this respect the swing of expenditure towards sales promotion has, in part, represented an improvement in the productivity of marketing budgets. Some of the money is being spent more efficiently.

SHORT-TERMISM

Unfortunately it's equally true that one of the oldest and most dangerous lessons learned has been that certain forms of sales promotion can increase sales dramatically in the immediate short term. This creates a temptation to respond to any decline in brand share by mounting a quick promotion to give sales an immediate boost. It's so much easier and quicker than addressing the fundamental problems that may have caused this decline in the brand's position.

In the short term this may make the originator of the promotion an instant hero. But the long-term consequences for the brand may be grave, if in practice it becomes reliant on ever more frequent, ever more expensive promotional boosts, to maintain a user-franchise no longer based on the brand's inherent values and appeals.

The most common form this short-termism takes is price-cutting and discounting. And in many countries these represent the largest part of all expenditure on sales promotion.

This temptation to use sales promotion for short-term sales increases is at its greatest when responsibility for promotional matters is left in the hands of junior managers who are advancing quickly up the organizational ladder. They may well spend only a year or so assigned to a particular brand. They are keen to demonstrate their ability to produce an 'improvement' in the brand's position. Increased sales are the most clearly observable evidence of 'improvement'. If price-cutting is the quickest way to achieve higher sales, then there will be more price-cutting. They will have moved on up to their next job, before the erosion of brand values, which may result, begins to show through in declining profits.

DISTRIBUTOR POWER

Across Europe the past 25 years have also witnessed a rapid concentration in the ownership of wholesale and retail outlets, affecting more and more business sectors.

It is now commonplace for outlets which account for half of all sales of a branded product or service to be owned or controlled by less than ten retail chains – sometimes by as few or two or three.

The individual retail chain is often much more important as a customer to the brand, than the brand is to the chain. The chain may handle perhaps 15 per cent of the brand's total national sales, but the brand may represent only 1 per cent of the chain's total turnover, since the chain handles many other suppliers' products or services too.

Distributors' ability to negotiate the terms and conditions on which they retail suppliers' products and services has thus been greatly strengthened. And an important form in which this power has been exercised has been distributors' demands for promotional support – support which suppliers often feel impelled to agree to and to finance.

The outcome has been a further boost to promotional expenditure.

EUROPEAN CASE STUDIES

Chapters 2 to 8, inclusive, which follow, contain case studies of sales promotions that have been mounted in individual European countries in the 1980s and early 1990s. Chapter 9 consists of studies of promotions that have crossed national boundaries, appearing in a number of different European countries.

In all cases the selection is the author's personal choice, designed to exemplify sales promotion playing a number of different roles effectively. However, the very large majority of the promotions described here have also won awards for excellence, in their own countries and on occasion at an international level.

Appendix C provides information on the approximate populations of individual countries and the exchange rate values of their currencies, to assist the reader in understanding the relative scale of numbers and costs quoted in these case studies.

ADVANTAGES OF THE CASE STUDY APPROACH

'Sales promotion' is a term which covers a very broad spectrum of marketing activities. It includes a wide variety of promotional techniques, most of which are illustrated in this book. General statements about sales promotion are therefore difficult to make with accuracy and precision. To be valid they are best arrived at pragmatically, from a study of the particular, from looking closely at individual promotions and seeing what general conclusions may be deduced from actual experience.

GROUPING BY OBJECTIVES

All successful business is objective-oriented, so the main grouping of the case studies which follow is therefore by objective – what the promotions were trying to achieve.

Other secondary classifications may be of interest to certain readers. Sales promotion specialists, for example, may wish to refer quickly to the uses made of an individual sales promotion technique; readers involved in the marketing of postal services may wish to turn first to examples of promotion in this sector; those about to enter a new European market may wish to look up examples of promotions in that country.

All these classifications and cross-references are facilitated by the index at the end of the book.

WHO SHOULD READ THIS BOOK?

This book is directed at all marketing and sales personnel who use – or intend to use – sales promotion to achieve their business objectives. This means people who value the insights to be gained, and the lessons to be learned, from a study of other companies' experiences; people who are specifically concerned with marketing and selling across national frontiers; or people who are simply alert to the possibility that what is happening in Italy or France today may happen in the UK tomorrow – or vice versa – and that a blinkered, single-country approach to sales promotion (or indeed any other aspect of business) is no longer entirely adequate.

2

AWARENESS

Introduction

Making people aware of a product or service is a task that older textbooks on marketing assigned to media advertising and public relations. Advertising in particular, so the theory went, would register a brand name in the audience's mind, explain what the brand did and what its competitive advantages were, and create a desire for it. Sales promotion's role was seen as helping convert this awareness, under-standing and desire into an actual purchase.

This theory was never more than partially valid, and it has become less and less adequate as an explanation of how things happen. Today, people become aware of brands in many different ways. Self-service and open display shops, which now dominate all forms of retailing in Europe, are an important source of information as to which brands are available. Word of mouth is another, allied to observing a member of a peer group using a particular brand.

Sales promotion, too, can play a central role in improving awareness. Sales promotion can communicate, as well as offer inducements. Here are some examples.

THE GREAT NIKE SOCCER BOOT TRANSFER

GROSSER NIKE FUSSBALLSCHUHTRANSFER

BACKGROUND

The Germans are great players of sports. At an international level they excel in a number of them: no nation can equal the record of the German team in the soccer World Cup in recent decades.

The market for sporting equipment in Germany is correspondingly large, and fiercely competitive. German manufacturers such as Adidas and Puma have expanded to achieve dominant positions in many other countries too.

In the domestic German market Nike is a successful and well-known brand in sports such as tennis, athletics and basketball. As a supplier of soccer gear, however, it was little known until recently, this soccer market being dominated by Adidas and Puma. A range of Nike football boots had been introduced in 1988, but with low levels of marketing support, resulting in a low level of consumer awareness.

By the autumn of 1990 it was becoming urgent to make the German public realize that Nike was now a force in soccer too. It was becoming equally urgent to provide evidence to sports retailers that they were right to continue stocking Nike soccer boots – and that, given support, they could move them off the shelves!

SPONSORSHIP

The first step was to associate Nike with soccer more strongly.

A contract with Borussia Dortmund was signed to sponsor this leading team. As a result the team wore Nike soccer boots and carried the Nike logo on their shirts throughout the 1990/1 season.

Andy Möller, one of the most popular players in the German league, was also signed up to represent Nike and to help test new products.

SALES PROMOTION

Soccer shoes are not a frequent purchase! A new pair is bought only occasionally: to prepare for a new season, because the existing pair has worn out; because a boy's feet have grown too large for the old ones; or because there's now something new and better available.

The Great Nike Soccer Transfer – boots instead of players!

New boots are not bought while watching a match or reading an advertisement – they're bought in sports shops! And usually the purchase will involve examining the alternatives available there and trying on different pairs. A brand which is prominently displayed will suggest there's something special about it. A recommendation by the shop staff may influence the final decision.

Nike needed to achieve this in-store prominence if it was to challenge the strong position of Adidas and Puma. And it needed to gain the confidence and support of sports retailers.

Sales promotion provided the means for them to do this.

Consumers were invited to take part in the soccer 'transfer' market – to transfer not a player but their boots! They were invited to swap their old boots for a new pair of Nike.

The old boots were brought into the shop. Their value was estimated by the dealer and this amount was offered as an immediate discount on the price of a new pair of Nike boots.

The old boots were then tossed into a transparent container which had above it a header card announcing the offer. The vast majority of these old boots were Adidas and Puma, powerfully communicating the theme that Nike was the new star in everybody's team. And the message was communicated not just in words and pictures (the tools of media advertising), but with actual soccer boots.

This excellent display also carried a card dispenser. The cards invited consumers to telephone a number and quote the Nike slogan ('Just do it'). Correct slogans qualified for entry in a draw to win tickets for a European Cup match or runners-up prizes of footballs signed by Borussia Dortmund players. This was further evidence of Nike's close association with soccer at its highest level, and a further opportunity for the consumer to be involved with Nike.

The promotion lasted for two months, at the end of which Nike collected the old soccer boots from dealers and disposed of them. Dealers were credited with the discounts they had given, at a standard, prearranged rate.

OTHER MEDIA SUPPORT

Commercials on all German radio stations helped communicate the offer.

It was also announced in the largest circulation magazine in Germany, *Stern*. Regional editions listed participating dealers in the local area on half pages facing the standard full page.

In addition to in-store displays, dealers were supplied with advertisements personalized to their stores, for them to place in local newspapers, and also mailing materials for them to send to their previous customers, football clubs and similar prospects.

Results

The Great Nike Soccer Boot Transfer was a great success.

Prior to the promotion the market share of Nike soccer boots stood at 2 per cent, compared with 60 per cent for Adidas and 30 per cent for Puma. After the promotion the Nike figure had increased to 10 per cent.

Before the promotion only 200 dealers stocked Nike soccer boots. However, 800 participated in the promotion, using the displays provided. Telephone interviews with these participating dealers indicated strong and enthusiastic approval of the promotion.

Approximately 40,000 consumers accepted the offer of 'transferring' their old boots for a new Nike pair.

Approximately 10,000 telephone calls were received, nearly all of them correctly quoting the Nike slogan.

A sales target was set at a level approximately 500 per cent higher than for the same two months a year earlier. In the event sales were almost double this target.

Nike is now clearly established in the target market's mind as a leading brand for soccer, as well as tennis, athletics and basketball shoes.

Agency: Pfriem & Partner

COMMENT

A most imaginative use of space in retail outlets to create awareness – and sales!

Your Income Tax is Cancelled!

Les Impôts sur le Revenu sont Supprimés!

Background

Heudebert markets a range of rusks and toasted breads (croustillants) *in France. It's a wide range, including:*

- *Triscotte;*
- *Le Pain Pelletier;*
- *Le Villageois;*
- *Le P'tit Grillé;*
- *Grany;*
- *Biscottes;*
- *Braisor;*
- *Croquine etc.*

This was a richer and more varied range than most French consumers were fully aware of.

In 1986 a decision was taken to promote the whole range under the umbrella theme 'Have a better life every day with Heudebert' ('Vivre tous les jours mieux avec Heudebert'). Promote, rather than advertise, since as we shall see it has been sales promotion events that have carried the main responsibility for supporting these products – classic advertising media such as press and television have been employed only to help communicate promotional offers.

The first promotion to put into effect this theme was a striking offer of 'Take a year off work – Heudebert will pay your salary!' ('Un an de salaire pour une année sabbatique') – a chance to win a dream prize for those working women who represented a key target market.

The promotion was successful: sales of Heudebert croustillants *advanced by 11.5 per cent in 1986, compared with an increase of only 3.5 per cent in the total market.*

Encouraged by this success another attention-grabbing promotional theme was created for the following year.

Your income tax is cancelled – for two years!

THE CONSUMER PROMOTION

In France, 28 February is the last date by which annual income tax returns must be made. As the date draws close income tax is uppermost in everyone's mind.

The day before 28 February this 'teaser' message appeared on half pages in national newspapers: 'YOUR INCOME TAX IS CANCELLED!', followed by an invitation to learn more by watching the TF1 television channel at 11.00 pm the following evening.

This 'teaser' worked: the audience for TF1 at the specified time was 20 per cent larger than normal. It saw a long, 15-minute commercial which revealed all: 'HEUDEBERT OFFERS YOU TWO YEARS WITHOUT TAXES!' – a cheque for between FFr 30,000 and 70,000, depending on the individual's tax liability. There were runners-up prizes of car maintenance and insurance for a year, financing of a year's leisure-time activities, and FFr 50 refunds on the Heudebert range. All of these were designed to help 'Have a better life every day with Heudebert'.

The commercial explained the rules of the contest in which these prizes were to be won: consumers were required to match names and pictures of Heudebert products. The chance of winning these prizes was made more credible by featuring the winner of the previous year's 'Take a Year Off Work' contest. And this long TV spot provided ample opportunities to present the whole range of Heudebert rusks and toasted breads.

Twelve million Heudebert packs carrying the promotional message were sold into the shops following this TV announcement. And the offer received further powerful support in national newspapers (10 million circulation), TV programme magazines (30 million circulation) and point of purchase displays.

All these media explained that winners would be drawn on a live television programme on 20 June.

SALES FORCE

These announcements to the consumer were preceded by a teaser mailing to the Heudebert sales force. This took the form of a letter in the exact typographical style and layout of communications from the Ministry of Finance, informing salespeople that income taxes were to be cancelled, and inviting them to ring a toll-free telephone number to hear more details.

Their attention was engaged immediately and the phone lines were kept busy! Salespeople experienced for themselves just how intriguing the message to the consumer was going to prove and how much impact it would have.

RETAIL TRADE

Twelve hundred managers of large food outlets received a newsletter describing the success of the previous year's promotion, describing the new promotion, detailing the scheme whereby a prize of a coffee machine would be awarded to a shopper in each store and inviting them to participate themselves in a lottery to win a range of executive gifts.

The newsletter was designed in the style of a TV programme magazine, and store managers were urged to watch the Heudebert 15-minute spot on the evening of 28 February.

PR

Teasers were mailed to journalists, inviting them to attend the 'première' screening of the Heudebert TV spot in the TF1 television studios.

Results

Seven hundred thousand consumers participated in the promotion.

The number of in-store displays was 50 per cent more than had been set as an objective.

Spontaneous and prompted consumer awareness of the full Heudebert range improved.

Heudebert sales increased by 5.8 per cent in 1987, compared with an overall market growth of 3.5 per cent.

The promotion received widespread editorial comment in the media. The marketing manager of Heudebert and the agency general manager were interviewed live on television.

Agency: Edi Conseil (now ECCLA)

COMMENT

This promotion has a number of excellent features.

To achieve wide-scale awareness it locks on to an external 'event' already uppermost in the mind of the French public at large: the need to make income tax returns by 28 February.

It gains strong attention by offering relief from the burden that tax represents for all of us.

It makes effective 'interactive' use of different media: the teaser press campaign increasing the audience for the television commercial the following evening.

The draw of winners is dramatized by being shown live to a national TV audience.

The theme and presentation of the promotion attracts media attention and comment, building further awareness.

The sales force and the distributive trade, whose co-operation and support are required to ensure the effective implementation of the promotion, are fully involved from the outset.

A nationwide promotion is 'personalized' to 1200 major stores, ensuring the support of these important outlets.

The promotion illustrates a promotional strategy at work, building on the success of the previous year's promotion and exploiting the same promotional theme, but with a different creative execution.

Full marks!

THE NEW VETRIL GAME SHOW

IL GIOCO DI NUOVO VETRIL

BACKGROUND

Vetril, manufactured by Brill, is the brand leader in the Italian market for window cleaners.

New Vetril was introduced in 1989. It was formulated to act as a multipurpose household cleaner, while still delivering a first-class result on windows.

The need was to make Italian housewives aware that Vetril was now 'new', and to communicate this extended range of uses for the brand.

THE PROMOTION

'*Look for the sparkle – hunt the diamond'. Vetril sponsored this TV game show in Italy*

A linked promotion was mounted both at the point of purchase and on sponsored television.

Display cards and collarettes on New Vetril bottles announced the 'New Vetril Game' at the point of purchase. Each week, for nine consecutive weeks, a diamond worth approximately 5 million lire was offered as a prize in a lottery. To enter the housewife simply wrote her name and address on the collarette, validated her entry by affixing a proof of purchase from the bottle label and mailed it in.

On television the daily programme *Dear Parents (Cari Genitori)* was sponsored for the same nine weeks. This quiz programme features parents and their children, recruited from the general public, playing against other competing families.

During the programme, parents are invited to answer questions on various topics and to write their answers on a blackboard. Their children, who remain outside the studio while this is going on, then come in and are posed the same questions. The process is then repeated, this time the children writing their answers on a blackboard while their parents are out of the studio. The aim is to get matching answers.

The main game during the nine-week sponsorship period was the New Vetril Game. The mechanics followed the usual format. A first general question concerning three different rooms – kitchen, living room and bathroom – was posed to parents or children. If their answers corresponded they won a prize in the form of gold coins. Gold coins not won that day were carried forward and added to the next day's prize fund.

Parents and children winning coins qualified to participate in the second stage of this New Vetril Game. Every day three different objects were taken from the kitchen, the living room and the bathroom and shown to the families, who then had to guess in which one New Vetril had hidden a diamond. The three rooms then appeared on the screen and a bottle of New Vetril passed across the room containing the diamond, leaving a trail of sparkling stars behind it. If the family had identified the correct room, the diamond was theirs!

Any diamonds not won in these television programmes were carried forward to the end of the nine-week promotion (together with coins not won in the last programme) and offered in a final lottery in which all the housewives who had sent in collarettes from the New Vetril bottle were entered. In addition, a truly spectacular diamond, worth L 100 million, was offered in this final lottery.

A further strong link was made between the sponsored TV and the point of purchase promotion. Each day, at the end of the transmission the TV programme's presenter announced a different 'sparkling' code word. Housewives who, by watching the programme, could write this code word on their collarette entry (together with the date of the programme's transmission) doubled the value of any prize they won: two diamonds instead of one.

Results

Just over 4 per cent of the collarettes were sent in as entries.

Of these approximately 80 per cent stated the code word written down from the TV programme.

Agency: Team 77.

COMMENT

TV quiz programmes such as *Cari Genitori* are enormously popular in Italy. A prime-time Saturday quiz, *Fantastico*, broadcast on the state-owned RAI channel, regularly achieves an audience of eight million viewers during the autumn and winter. *TeleMike*, featuring a universally-known personality, Mike Bongiorno, pulls in six million viewers on Canale 5, a privately owned channel. *Cari Genitori*, also on Canale 5, averages audiences of about 2.4 million, of which approximately 58 per cent are women. This is a considerable audience given that *Cari Genitori* is a daily programme broadcast around two o'clock in the afternoon.

It's the Italians who have pioneered this remarkable use of quiz programmes to promote brands. It all started in the early 1980s, with the liberalization of TV in Italy. Until then the state-owned channels had restricted advertising time and had not allowed programme sponsorship. The first of the private stations, Berlusconi's Fininvest channels, led the way by offering popular Saturday evening shows to sponsors, and very soon big advertisers, including the major detergent brands, were developing the format exemplified by this New Vetril Game.

Response rates were often enormous, especially in the early days, For example, a sponsored TV promotion to launch a new yoghurt brand, Più, pulled 4 million entries over a 12-week period, representing 20 million proofs of purchase.

Today, response rates are typically much lower: the novelty factor has worn off for the Italian public. Sponsored TV promotions none the less continue to offer a very viable route for achieving high levels of awareness for a brand, and for interactively linking what is clearly a very involving viewing experience for Italian audiences, with promotion at the point of purchase.

Promoters in other countries, where television sponsorship is liberalized, have or will have much technical expertise to learn from their Italian counterparts in this area.

Many other European countries could also learn something to their advantage from the Italians' relaxed attitude to commercial lotteries. It's entirely legal to require consumers to provide proof of purchase to enter a promotion in which prizes are awarded by lot, or chance. Nobody seems to come to any harm as a result, and why the state and legislature should forbid such promotional lotteries in other countries remains a puzzle.

Less to be emulated is the Italian requirement that such promotions must have authorization from a government ministry. Indeed between 1938 and 1988 the ministry issued an annual list of products which were allowed to be promoted. Many products such as bread, milk, pasta, edible oils, butter and mineral water were regularly excluded from these lists (which is why 'permitted' brands such as detergents were the first big users of TV sponsorship). Similarly, a ban in Italy on offering cash as a promotional reward does not seem to have much rationale. It's difficult to see what 'public interest' is at stake – particularly as the ban is commonly avoided by stating the cash value of the gold coins (*gettoni*) which are offered instead, as in this New Vetril Game. Legal restrictions on sales promotion are discussed further in Chapter 10.

In a number of respects the New Vetril Game represents a very sophisticated piece of communication. The prize of a diamond is both attractive in itself and it conveys the 'sparkling' results delivered by New Vetril. The Italian word for diamond is '*brillante*', tying in nicely with the manufacturer's name, Brill and the surfaces cleaned with New Vetril become 'brillianti', best translated as 'so clean they sparkle'.

Hiding the diamond in one or other of the three rooms shown in the TV quiz show communicates the much-extended range of surfaces, throughout the house, which New Vetril is now equipped to clean.

The trail of stars which New Vetril leaves as it passes across the room where the Vetril *brillante* is hidden reiterates the sparkling results obtained by using the brand.

The New Vetril Game, as played live on television, follows exactly the normal quiz format of *Cari Genitori*, right down to the children writing their answers on a blackboard where their parents can't see what they've written. This is not, therefore, a commercial interrupting an entertainment programme: the New Vetril 'plug' is *part* of the entertainment.

Cari Genitori is a warm-hearted programme for family viewing. The mothers who appear on it are proud of their children, the children clearly enjoy easy-going relationships with their parents. As such the programme represents an excellent context in which to communicate the roles of New Vetril in helping the housewife create a clean and attractive home for the family.

NKR 100,000 FOR A DOUBLE-PAGE SPREAD

ERNST G MORTENSEN BETALER 100,000 KRONER FOR Å TA LIVET AV EN MYTE

BACKGROUND

Ernst G Mortensen, one of Norway's oldest publishing houses, publishes nine mass-market magazines. These magazines achieve large circulations, but in 1987 advertising revenues were down. In part this was symptomatic of a decline in advertising expenditure across all Norwegian media, but magazines were also being hard hit by competition for budgets from a plethora of local and national daily newspapers.

The problem was made worse by the poor creative quality of much of the advertising appearing in magazines. Advertisers and their agencies were discouraged from bringing new ads to the magazines. All the exciting new advertisements were going into newspapers.

Action was required to make the advertising business more aware of the opportunities offered by magazines. They were looking for something which would redirect their attention from dailies to weeklies.

Of the three key decision-making groups – agency creative departments, media buyers and their clients – creative personnel were identified as the prime target. A campaign was launched to stimulate their imaginations about the creative possibilities of magazine advertising, by encouraging them to think in terms of a classic – but underutilized – magazine format, the double-page spread.

THE PROMOTION

The Ernst G Mortensen annual award was created, taking the form of a handsome glass pencil mounted on a solid stone base, accompanied by a prize of NKr 100,000.

The award was offered for the most creative use of a magazine double-page spread, as judged by a jury of four top advertising professionals, two of them Norwegian and the other two foreigners, to provide an international perspective.

A prize for creativity, from Mortensen the Norwegian magazine publisher

Two thousand mailshots were sent to people involved with creative advertisements. The mailings enclosed a brochure announcing the award, with the challenging statement that 'There's an incredible amount of garbage being inserted in Norwegian weeklies!'. And to show what could be done, and to stimulate that competitive instinct, examples were included of some recent, more creative, uses of the double-page format. A similar brochure was inserted in Norway's main advertising trade paper.

Advertising agencies' clients are sometimes wary of ads designed to win awards: as hard-headed businesspeople they point out they're paying for advertisements to sell their products! And media buyers are rightly concerned with the cost effectiveness of their media schedules. Their interests were therefore catered for too: for a limited period a 20 per cent discount was offered on all double-page spreads booked in any of Ernst G Mortensen's nine titles.

Results

In the first year of this annual award the magazines' sales of double-page spreads doubled. They have remained at this high level since.

There was a most telling indication that these higher sales were attributable primarily to the awareness and attention generated by the award, rather than just the 20 per cent discount: sales of double page spreads in other publishers' magazines also increased! The following year, therefore, the award was extended to all Norwegian magazines.

Agency: Scaneco – Cato Johnson

COMMENT

Sometimes even advertising needs promoting!

MAKE A PHONE CALL FREE WITH JOHNNIE WALKER

LE TÉLÉPHONE GRATUIT DE JOHNNIE WALKER

BACKGROUND

Johnnie Walker Scotch whisky first appeared in 1830. Historically it was brand leader in France, but in 1988 it had fallen back to second place in what had become a very fragmented market. Even Ballantines, the best-selling brand, achieved a share of only 8.2 per cent in that year, followed by Johnnie Walker with 7.5 per cent, Label 5 with 6.6 per cent, J&B with 6.2 per cent and Glen Campbell with 4.5 per cent. Half the French market, the third largest in the world for Scotch whisky consumption after the US and the UK, was accounted for by miscellaneous 'all other' brands.

Johnnie Walker sales had been declining for two years, during which it had received hardly any advertising support and very little promotion. However, responsibility for distributing the brand passed to Moët Hennessy Distribution in 1988, and a fundamental review of its marketing was initiated. Attention was concentrated on Johnnie Walker Red Label, which competes in the large sector for Scotch whiskies aged for less than 12 years, representing 74 per cent of the total French whisky market.

Several related problems became clear. While prompted *awareness of Johnnie Walker was higher than for any other whisky brand, at 72 per cent, it was a very passive and unfocused awareness. The public were not able to give any coherent account of what the brand stood for. It was just part of the 'wallpaper', the background 'scenery'. And, not surprisingly in view of the near-absence of strong marketing support in recent years, this was especially the case with younger potential consumers in the 25–35-year-old age group. They had grown up vaguely knowing of Johnnie Walker, but not doing anything about it!*

Particularly worrying was the very poor distribution of the brand in locations such as cafés, bars, restaurants, hotels and nightclubs ('CHR' outlets), where whiskies are consumed on the premises. While these outlets account for only 31 per cent of Scotch whisky sales in France (compared with 57 per cent selling through supermarkets and hypermarkets), they are important in creating positive awareness of a brand. Visitors observe members of their peer group – perhaps even a role model – drinking a certain brand and follow their example. Favourable experience of the brand in CHR locations in turn leads to its purchase from supermarkets and hypermarkets for consumption at home.

The urgent need, therefore, was to create a much sharper, focused and active awareness of Johnnie Walker Red Label, in particular among younger consumers in the 25–35-year-old age group, and similarly in cafés, bars, restaurants, hotels and nightclubs.

A classic media advertising campaign was considered unlikely to achieve this breakthrough with the required speed and impact. Instead, a high-profile promotional activity was selected.

APPELEZ VOS AMIS AVEC JOHNNIE WALKER:

CE SOIR LE TELEPHONE EST GRATUIT.

05 70 10 10

APPEL GRATUIT

Make a phone call free – anywhere in the world!

THE CONSUMER OFFER

On Saturday 19 November 1988, the French public received an announcement guaranteed to make them sit up and take notice: 'This evening you can make a phone call FREE!'

Better still the phone call could be to *anywhere in the world*, regardless of distance. The only restrictions were that the call should be made between 9 o'clock that evening and midnight, and that it should be limited to two minutes in length. This was a great opportunity to ring a friend – with the compliments of Johnnie Walker.

This attention-grabbing message was communicated on the day in half-page two-colour spaces in the 'opinion-forming' national newspapers *Le Monde, Libération, L'Équipe, Le Figaro,* and by frequent spots on the Europe 1 and NRJ radio networks.

The same media schedule was employed to give advance warning of this generous offer the day before: 'Ring your friends to let them know that tomorrow they can make a phone call FREE!'.

OPERATIONAL ASPECTS

Pioneering promotions such as this frequently need new facilities to be developed – ways of doing things which had not previously existed. Great promotional concepts can go badly wrong in practice if they're not backed up with meticulous attention to operational detail.

The number quoted in this offer of a free call was 'freephone' (*un numéro 'vert'*) – a service readily available from the French telephone network, France Télécom. So far so good. The problem was that France Télécom had no facilities for passing this type of call to another subscriber. Specialist telephone marketing companies, too, could handle either outgoing or incoming calls, but only very rarely could they offer the required combination of both, ie receiving a call and passing it on.

The solution was to introduce an operator as a friendly third party to the conversation. The line remained open on the operator's switchboard for the duration of the call, and this necessity was turned to good commercial advantage. The operator introduced the call by explaining to the recipient that it was complimentary from Johnnie Walker, and finished the call by playing a recording of the Johnnie Walker jingle.

Two specialist telemarketing companies, Phone Marketing and Téléperformance, were recruited to provide 200 switchboard operators. This was a wise precaution, since otherwise the number of calls made during this intensive three-hour period would have 'blown the fuse' of France Télécom's normal *numéro vert* service.

THE SALES FORCE

The Moët Hennessy sales force needed early forewarning of the promotion if they were to exploit the sales opportunities it presented.

The day before they were due to set out for their annual conference in Scotland, in September, all sales personnel (approximately 150) received through the post a small, cordless telephone with a simple but urgent message: 'Ring this freephone number NOW!'. They did so, and were given a verbal outline of this unusual promotion to be launched in November. Full details followed at the conference.

CAFÉS, HOTELS AND RESTAURANTS

France has some 13,000 locations where alcoholic drinks are consumed on the premises. Seven thousand of these were carefully selected as being good potential outlets for Johnnie Walker, and were mailed with details of the promotion and – of course – the offer of a free phone call to anywhere in the world.

Two hundred nightclubs and discotheques received special attention, since these are the places where 25–35 year olds pick up much information on what's 'in': the new fashions in music, dancing, clothes, slang and drinking. Salespeople invited these 200 outlets to take part in an 'unprecedented promotional event': by offering their clientele the opportunity to phone a friend anywhere in the world *from their table*, FREE, thanks to Johnnie Walker. Cordless telephones were supplied, boxed in a cardboard model of the traditional red British phone booth which announced the offer to customers. On the evenings of Friday 18 and 25 November proprietors of the nightclubs and discos put these out on tables where they were doing a good trade in drinks.

TAKE-HOME TRADE

Supermarket and hypermarket managers were invited to make their own free calls, no matter where, on evenings reserved for them, 3, 8 and 14 November, in advance of the consumer offer.

Point of purchase draws were held for shoppers in individual hypermarkets, to win mini cordless telephones.

PR

Four hundred journalists received through the mail a bottle of Johnnie Walker Red Label Scotch whisky, a mini cordless telephone, full details of the consumer promotion and an invitation to make their own free telephone call.

POST-PROMOTION FOLLOW-UP

Everybody who had participated in the promotion on 19 November was thanked by Johnnie Walker on 21 November, in quarter-page two-colour spaces in the same newspapers as had been used to announce the offer. Too often promotions neglect such small courtesies, which can significantly enhance the goodwill generated by the actual offer.

Results

Eight hundred thousand free telephone calls were made between 9.00 pm and midnight on 19 November. Sixty five per cent of them were overseas calls.

Reports from switchboard operators indicate that a large part of many telephone conversations was concerned with discussing the fact that Johnnie Walker was financing the call.

The promotion received extensive editorial coverage in press and broadcast media.

Sales of Johnnie Walker Red Label in November were the highest ever recorded, and sales continued to be buoyant in the first half of the following year.

Agency: Edi Conseil (now ECCLA)

COMMENT

This promotion is an excellent example of a simple, powerful concept being vigorously exploited through all commercial channels to all target audiences. Its success resulted as much from perspiration as from the original inspiration.

The very high prompted awareness of Johnnie Walker, at a time when sales were none the less declining, illustrates that awareness itself is of limited value to a brand if it is diffuse, unfocused and passive in character. Putting friends in touch with each other by telephone was entirely consistent with the shared conviviality that Johnnie Walker had been in the business of stimulating since 1830. In this respect the promotion sharpened perceptions of what the brand stands for, enhanced the brand image – a role for sales promotion which we shall examine more fully in Chapter 5.

3

SAMPLING AND TRIAL

INTRODUCTION

In many well-established product categories inertia plays a big part in determining consumer choices between brands. A brand may be bought out of habit as much as for any more thought-out reason, or it could be that the reasons which made the brand right for the consumer when it was first chosen have subsequently been subsumed into what has now become a habit.

Individual consumers change over time, however: their tastes evolve. Brands, too, undergo development. A brand and one of its long-term loyal consumers may begin to move in different directions, follow new interests, but without either quite noticing the changes in each other. They've got used to each other, they're comfortable with each other and they no longer examine each other's behaviour as closely as when they first came together.

An alternative brand, perhaps a new brand, may well suit this individual consumer's evolving tastes better. But for it to have any chance of displacing the incumbent brand, it will need to intrude itself into this existing cosy and undemanding relationship.

Sampling – the offering of a free sample – is the most intrusive of all marketing techniques. Rather than attempting to woo the consumer with love messages from the television screen or the pages of newspapers, sampling instead presents the consumer with the physical experience of the brand in use. This is an exceptionally forceful form of seduction.

Sampling, however, is usually a very expensive form of promotion, even when targeted as carefully as in the case studies which follow. This chapter therefore moves on to show examples of other techniques also being used successfully to achieve trial.

LÖWENBRÄU BAVARIAN SHORTS

BACKGROUND

Löwenbräu, originating in Munich, is today one of the world's most famous brands of lager beer. In Britain it is brewed under licence and distributed by Allied Breweries, one of the top four suppliers of the UK beer market. In view of its justified prestige in other countries, Allied Breweries sensibly chose the brand as their entrant in the premium-price sector of the UK lager market.

By the middle 1980s, however, Löwenbräu was in serious danger of failing in this country. In 1985 Löwenbräu UK sales fell back by 2 per cent at a time when lager sales advanced overall by 18 per cent, year on year. The explanations were not difficult to seek: the brand's image was weak and diffuse among British lager drinkers; its taste was considered bland; and its alcoholic strength was low for a premium brand.

These problems were addressed by a major relaunch of the brand in mid 1986. 'New improved Löwenbräu strong lager' was now brewed at a higher original gravity of 1047° and this greater strength was signalled on a redesigned counter dispense unit. The beer was given a more distinctively continental taste. A new advertising campaign emphasized Löwenbräu's Bavarian pedigree, while satirizing the more risible aspects of Bavarian life – 'Thankfully they sent us their lager, not their shorts' – the British never having been able to comprehend how grown men could bring themselves to wear lederhosen.

To complete this relaunch package a promotion was required which would induce lager drinkers to experience Löwenbräu for themselves in this improved form.

THE PROMOTION

Approximately 7000 pubs and clubs were supplied with mini Bavarian steins and point of purchase displays offering consumers 'Free Bavarian Shorts' – not *lederhosen*, but a mini stein of Löwenbräu to try free.

Allied Breweries financed the supply of free Löwenbräu sufficient for samples to be dispensed over two weeks, on average, in each participating outlet.

Sampling Löwenbräu Strong Lager

Results

The 2 per cent per annum decline in Löwenbräu's UK sales before the relaunch was turned round into a 60 per cent increase in the year following.

The new advertising campaign was withdrawn soon after the relaunch, in the light of a negative research report. The new counter dispenser unit and this sales promotion therefore took the main responsibility for successfully communicating the characteristics of the new, stronger, improved Löwenbräu, providing an impetus for the brand's growth through sampling opportunities.

During the following two years the 'Free Bavarian Shorts' promotion was employed to open new accounts in the 'free trade' sector (ie outlets not in any way 'tied' to a particular brewer).

The fast-growing sales of Löwenbräu in pubs and clubs formed the platform for the brand's successful launch subsequently in take-home outlets.

Agency: The Core Group

COMMENT

Mini steins are attractive and intriguing objects for any beer lover to handle. They have something of the same appeal as miniature bottles of spirits, which some drinkers collect rather than consume. The analogy with spirits is apt too, since the smallness of the mini stein conveys the alcoholic strength of Löwenbräu in its relaunched form. 'Shorts' is sometimes used as a synonym for measures of strong spirits.

Moreover, the dispensing of free samples in these very small mini steins suggests Löwenbräu is valuable and expensive – good support for the brand's premium price.

Of course, some of these free samples will be wasted: they will be asked for by customers who are not likely to take up drinking a strong lager such as Löwenbräu, but who are happy to get anything for nothing. Such wastage was an acceptable price to pay, however, to reach a large number of genuine prospects in the places where they do their drinking; at a time when their presence in the pub indicates they need a drink; with a simple, uncluttered and powerful inducement to try the brand in its new form.

Ambassadors for Senior Citizens' Rail Cards

NS Senioren Ambassadeurs Van Seniorenkaart

Background

Like other European train operators Netherlands Railways (NS) offers older travellers a number of privileges. Those over 60 years of age qualify to buy a Senior Citizens' Rail Card, costing DFl70 and valid for one year. The Rail Card entitles the holder to 40 per cent reductions on fares, plus entirely free rail travel on seven days during the year. Additional rail travel by retired senior citizens puts seats on trains to good use, which otherwise would have stayed empty during off-peak periods.

In its present form this Senior Citizens' Rail Card dates from 1985, when the Netherlands Railways sold approximately 350,000. This was considered a very satisfactory achievement, making the scheme a success, by European comparisons. However, the Dutch Central Bureau of Statistics calculated there were approaching two and a half million over 60s in Holland, and while clearly some of these were not prospects for rail travel for a variety of reasons, including incapacities, there none the less seemed to be potentially a bigger market for the Rail Card.

The key problem was how to target communication accurately and cost-effectively at these over 60s. The Senior Citizens' Rail Card had been publicized to some extent by booklets, posters and advertisements, but advertising in large circulation magazines and newspapers was, for example, very wasteful since most readers were under 60.

Direct mail looked a promising route in theory, but in practice no available database in Holland identified those who were over 60. And – worse still – the Netherlands Railways had not captured by any means all the names and addresses of current Senior Citizen Rail Card holders, many of whom paid for their cards at local provincial rail stations throughout the country. If any form of inducement to buy a Rail Card was going to be offered there would be no way of knowing whether the recipients were already satisfied Rail Card holders, happy to renew their subscriptions without needing any inducement to do so.

A more thorough identification and screening of prospects was needed.

THE PROMOTION

In July 1986 approximately 6000 retired former employees of the Netherlands Railways were invited, by mail, to assist in a promotion to recruit new Senior Citizen Rail Card holders. NS's mailing list of these retired employees was complete and up to date.

In October those accepting this invitation were sent three large envelopes to pass on to friends of their own generation who had not yet realized the benefits and value-for-money available from the Senior Citizen Rail Card.

Each envelope contained a selection of small gifts: coupons for a free newspaper, a free cup of coffee and a discount on a bunch of flowers; a copy of a newspaper published twice a year for senior citizens, *Seniorenwijzer;* a leaflet describing the benefits of the Senior Citizen Rail Card; and – most important of all – a trial Rail Card, valid for two months.

A covering letter invited the recipient to 'be the guest of the Netherlands Railways' for the next two months by filling in his name and address on the application form attached to the trial Rail Card, and handing it in at the nearest railway station ticket office for it to be date-stamped and validated.

The retired NS employees who had made the introduction received a 'thank you' letter and a complimentary copy of the latest railway timetable. At the end of the 2-month 'sampling' period their friends received a letter encouraging them to subscribe for a full 12-month Senior Citizen Rail Card.

Senior Citizen Rail Cards were sampled by the Netherlands Railways

Results

Of the 6000 retired NS employees invited to assist only 1000 had been expected to accept. In practice 3600 did so.

Each received three envelopes to pass on to friends: ie 10,800 prospects.

Then, 6100 of these 10,800 used the trial Rail Card. And 1200 of them bought a full, 12-month Senior Citizen Rail Card at the end of the 2-month trial period.

In 1987 sales of the cards increased by 13,000 to 377,000, one-tenth of this increase being directly attributable to this promotion.

The promotion was repeated on a larger scale in 1988, with sales of cards rising towards 400,000.

A pay-back calculation indicated that the cost of the 1986/7 promotion was more than twice covered by the revenue generated by the 1200 new card holders it recruited.

Agency: Bridge KLP

COMMENT

Retired employees of the Netherlands Railways were perfect distributors of this sampling promotion, perfect ambassadors for the Rail Card. Who better positioned to identify those likely to be interested from among their circles of acquaintances; who better equipped to answer questions about the railways?

Their enthusiasm for their former employer was indicated by their high level of acceptance (60 per cent) of the invitation to help mount this promotion.

THE ART OF LOVING COFFEE

L'ART D'AIMER LE CAFÉ

BACKGROUND

Nescafé in France offers a wide selection of coffee types and flavours: in 1986 there were ten to choose from.

In practice many French coffee drinkers tend to be a little conservative, stocking just one or two favourite coffees in the kitchen at home. And few of even a more experimental minority would have tried all ten Nescafé varieties.

As Nescafé was the only soluble coffee brand to offer some of these flavours it had a strong interest in creating a taste and demand for them.

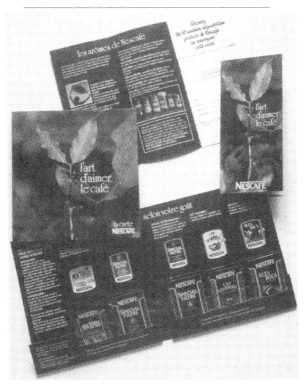

Nescafé taught 'The Art of Loving Coffee' with these samples

THE PROMOTION

In autumn 1986 ten million homes in France received through their letterboxes a leaflet entitled 'The Art of Loving Coffee'. It described the pleasures of coffee drinking and in particular the subtly different pleasures of different coffee beans: Columbian; Mocamban; Alta Rican etc.

The reader was invited to complete the application forming part of the leaflet and to mail it in to receive back sample sachets of all ten Nescafé varieties.

Results

Over 700,000 households (more than 7 per cent of the ten million which received the leaflet) applied for the free samples.

Agency: Caramel

COMMENT

Distributing the free-sample sachets to all ten million homes would have been both extremely expensive and very wasteful.

By requiring housewives to apply for them Nescafé filtered out households with no real interest in experimenting with new coffee flavours.

Moreover, one can argue that perhaps consumers tend to prize more highly – or at least pay closer attention to – something they have had to exert themselves to obtain.

Additionally, the brand obtained the names and addresses of prime prospects for further promotion of Nescafé.

IT'S TIME FOR A WILD WEEKEND

BACKGROUND

From its launch in 1970 Range Rover's great success was based on building a loyal franchise among customers needing a functional, four-wheel drive performance, but wanting to combine this with style and comfort.

By the middle 1980s the dividing line between utility vehicles and luxury saloon cars was becoming blurred, and it was apparent that Range Rover could potentially extend its market to include buyers who previously would have chosen perhaps a Jaguar, Mercedes or BMW.

For such people a Range Rover offered not only the functional advantages of a clearer view of the road and the freedom of the countryside, but also the aspirational appearance of being land owners and/or successful in their chosen careers.

The way forward was to give this new type of potential owner direct personal experience of the Range Rover's versatility, capabilities and luxury, in a suitably aspirational context.

A test drive 'round the block' was not sufficient. The need was to get potential customers behind the wheel for a sustained period, where the driving position was sure to grow on the prospect.

THE PROMOTION

Thirty-five thousand holders of Barclays Premier Cards received the following letter in October 1985 from the chief executive of this chargecard.

IT'S TIME FOR A WILD WEEKEND

I am pleased to announce an exclusive offer for Barclays Premier Cardholders, to sample the special capabilities of the 1986 Range Rover, with our compliments, for a winter weekend break in the country.

Not only are you being given the chance to experience the luxury and versatility of the new Range Rover, but you also have the opportunity to take advantage of a country break organized by Range Rover with Prestige Hotels, in the wilds of Britain. These hotel breaks offer you

IT'S TIME FOR A WILD WEEKEND

The complimentary use of a Range Rover for a weekend in the country luxurious accommodation, gourmet food and a special country pursuit at one of Britain's finest privately owned hotels. The country pursuits available range from clay pigeon shooting and coarse fishing to horse riding in some of the most beautiful country locations.

If you would like to take this opportunity to leave business life behind for the quiet of the country, simply contact your local Range Rover dealer who will arrange a convenient weekend for you to take possession of the Range Rover fuelled and ready to go. And if you wish, your dealer will also reserve the Prestige Hotel break of your choice.

Full details of this exclusive offer are carried in the accompanying folder.

This is a rare chance to have a weekend to remember in one of Britain's most prestigious cars.

The accompanying folder contained stunning photographs of the Range Rover in places quite inaccessible to a conventional luxury saloon car, and – looking equally 'right' – parked in front of some of the elegant country hotels participating in the offer. The hotel addresses were listed and pinpointed on a map; participating Range Rover dealers were listed; the plus points of the Range Rover were fully described. The Barclays Premier Cardholder needed to do no more than pick up a phone and speak to a dealer for the whole weekend to be arranged.

The socio-economic profile of the Barclays Premier Card list was right for Range Rover's purposes and, very importantly, this was the first time these cardholders had been exposed to a promotional mailing from the luxury car market sector.

The mailing was timed to reach cardholders the day before advertising broke for a new 'Vogue' model, offering even higher standards of luxury and on-road performance, and making the Range Rover even more attractive to the traditional driver of a luxury saloon car.

Results

Approximately 1750 Premier Cardholders booked these test drive weekends, three-quarters of them booking in at Prestige Hotels.

Range Rover sales in December were 17 per cent higher than a year earlier, and Range Rover's 25 per cent share of the luxury car market in that month was its highest ever.

Agency: Below The Line Projects

COMMENT

Even expensive consumer durables can be sampled!

TEST ITS COVERING POWER — IN ADVANCE!

BACKGROUND

Crown Paints knew that the premium price they were asking for their new 'Advance' range of emulsion paints was more than justified by its performance. Research had proved that Advance provided better than ever cover of the surface to be painted, in a single coat.

To convince the consumer, however, physical evidence of this dramatic performance needed to be provided at first hand.

Two trial techniques that have been used before in the paint sector were considered but rejected. Demonstrations by auxiliary sales staff in stores, or on a travelling 'roadshow', were going to be too expensive in relation to the limited number of potential consumers who would see a demonstration. The second technique, selling small pots of paint as samplers through stores, would again reach only that limited number of potential users who were willing to make the act of faith required to purchase even this small pot. Moreover, a tiny pot of emulsion paint has little practical use, whereas one of the attractions of similar-sized pots of gloss paint had always been that they could be used to cover a small surface, perhaps a door, or to retouch a damaged surface.

THE PROMOTION

'Mini-sampler' kits were made up containing a minute amount of Advance paint, a small paintbrush and a picture of a chequerboard pattern. Consumers were invited to examine for themselves Advance's cover power by applying a single coat to the chequerboard.

As a further inducement to do so a Rover Metro car was offered as a prize in a free draw, open to everybody who sent in a painted-out chequerboard.

Those consumers 'converted' by this demonstration of Advance's covering power and needing emulsion paint immediately could use the £1 coupon which formed part of the sampler kit.

Crown Advance samplers were distributed through the letterboxes of some two and a half million homes likely to engage in do-it-yourself decorating, in the catchment areas of major stores stocking Advance. In addition 600,000 samplers were covermounted on the magazines *Women's Realm* and *Practical Householder*.

TEST ITS COVERING POWER...*IN ADVANCE!*

...AND YOU COULD WIN A FANTASTIC ROVER METRO 1.1S

Plus £1 off your next purchase of Crown Advance

A sample and a brush to test the covering power of Crown Advance paint

Results

One hundred and twenty thousand painted-out chequerboards were received as entries for the free draw for the Metro car.

Approximately 15,000 £1 coupons were redeemed between issue in April 1991 and the closing date in August.

Agency: Beaumont Bennett

COMMENT

This is an example of how a painted-out picture is worth a thousand words!

At no cost to themselves consumers could test Advance's claims under their own control. And clearly very large numbers did so. A single Metro, just one, was not a particularly generous prize fund and the free draw represented more a polite 'thank you' from Crown Paints than an overpowering inducement. The fact that 4 per cent of those receiving a sampler none the less went to the trouble of sending in their painted-out chequerboards undoubtedly indicates that very many more had used them.

Similarly, the coupon redemption was quite brisk, given the short closing date and the fact that most householders would not have such an immediate need for emulsion paint. Home decoration is not an all-the-time activity for most of us!

JOHNSON WAX SHOE-SHINE BOYS

BACKGROUND

Johnson Wax One-Step shines any colour shoe in seconds. A demonstration of the results it achieves is impressive: demonstrations lead to sales.

In 1989, however, the UK marketing support budget was small: too small to finance demonstration by television advertising or by using employed demonstrators in the shops or streets, and certainly too small to pay for the widescale distribution of samples.

THE PROMOTION

Scouts and Cubs used Johnson Wax One-Step to shine shoes and raise money for their groups and packs, during the week commencing 3 April 1989.

The boys were supplied with free shoe-shine kits containing 24 pads of One-Step, a poster announcing the shoe-shine service and a full explanatory letter, including instructions on how to make a shoe-shine stand.

Six major retail customers agreed to allow Scouts/Cubs to shine shoes inside or outside their stores: Asda; Safeway; Presto; Gateway; Superdrug; and the Co-op (CRS).

One-Step was appointed official sponsor of this Scout 'Job Week', and the Scout sponsorship logo was printed on the One-Step pack.

While the main source of revenue for the Scouts and Cubs was the tips given to them by members of the public whose shoes were shined, Johnson Wax also donated cash prizes to the five groups who showed the most effective initiatives during this Job Week. Johnson Wax also offered a further £100 as the prize in a draw among all groups/packs who sent in press cuttings and other information about their shoe-shine activities (a reply-paid envelope for this purpose was included in the shoe-shine kit).

Scout groups and Cub packs were recruited to participate in the promotion by direct mail shots, an insert in the February 1989 issue of *Scouting* magazine and by an exhibition stand at the Scouts District Commissioners' conference.

Johnson Wax One-Step teamed up with the Scouts

Results

Over 4000 Scout groups/Cub packs participated, throughout the UK.

Over one million pairs of shoes were shined during the six days of the promotion.

And over £2 million was raised during the week for the Scouts Association.

The shoe-shining activities of more than 900 groups/packs were featured in their local press, or on local radio and television.

Agency: Promotional Campaigns

COMMENT

Everything falls into place when the starting point of a promotion is a strong, simple, relevant concept. This is a brilliant example.

Johnson Wax needed One-Step to be demonstrated, but had a budget sufficient only to fund demonstration materials. The Scouts needed to raise money from the public by doing jobs: shoe-shining represented a 'ready-made' job opportunity, once the necessary equipment was provided. Johnson Wax achieved a widescale demonstration of One-Step in a particularly favourable environment: an invitation to have your shoes shined is more likely to be accepted if it comes from a young Scout or Cub volunteer than from an adult, commercial demonstrator. The Scouts raised a great deal of money for their organization.

Everybody involved felt good – including the general public who had been pleased to 'tip' those young boys. Everybody involved was better off as a result of the promotion – again including the public, who now could see for themselves that there was a better way of shining their shoes.

WRITE TO ME

SCHRIJF MIJ

BACKGROUND

Private correspondence – writing letters to friends and relations – is in decline in Holland, as in most other 'developed' countries. This is particularly so with the younger generation, brought up in a world with easy access to telephones and with so many more ways available to them of employing their leisure time. Research indicates that young people enjoy receiving letters – it's writing them that they're not so keen about!

On the reasonable assumption that there's a positive link between the habit of reading and writing, the Dutch PTT Post embarked on a three-year sponsorship of the annual 'Children's Books Week', held every October by the prestigious Foundation for the Collective Promotion of the Dutch Book (CPNB). A whole range of activities are organized around children's books in schools, public libraries, bookshops and in the media, all round the country, with many authors participating.

In 1989 the theme was 'Look beyond the end of your nose, for new inventions and discoveries!'. It was this theme which provided the context for a sales promotion designed to give children aged 7 to 13 reasons to write letters, to show them that letter writing is easy and can be fun, and to provide them with addresses of like-minded children to write to.

THE PROMOTION

Children were invited to write a letter about their fantasy inventions to Paul Biegel. Paul Biegel is famous in Holland for his fairytale-like books for children and he was the author of the 'present' given to everyone buying a children's book during the 1989 Children's Books Week.

All letters were read carefully, and all received a reply from Paul Biegel. Enclosed with the reply was a booklet of tips and ideas for letters, 'Write to Me' notepaper, and three addresses of children of their own age who had also participated in the promotion; these addresses printed out on sticky labels.

The 25 children submitting the most imaginative fantasy inventions (judged in four separate age groups) received a *handwritten* letter from

'Write to Me' said this scheme to encourage Dutch children to correspond with each other

Paul Biegel. In an award ceremony he presented them with a 'Write to Me' certificate and a set of children's adventure books. Their winning letters were exhibited in the PTT Museum.

The promotion was announced on 11,000 posters in all primary schools in Holland and in the children's sections of public libraries. Leaflets were also distributed in libraries, an announcement of the promotion appeared on the back cover of *Kinderboekenmolen* (a magazine published in connection with Children's Books Week) and the promotion was advertised in three television programme guides.

Direct mail offered 1100 public libraries a kit (priced at Fls25) to help children write letters including, ideas, checklists, 'Write to Me' note-paper, a press release kit, envelopes etc.

During the campaign arrangements were made for schools who had begun spontaneously to collect their pupils' work to be linked with each other, to provide pen pals.

Results

Twenty-two thousand children wrote to Paul Biegel.

Four hundred and sixty (40 per cent) of the libraries accepted the mail-order offer of the letter-writing kit. They provided roughly half the number of children who participated.

The award ceremony for winners gained much free publicity, and the promotion generated a lot of goodwill for the Dutch PTT Post.

Research revealed the following:

- 96 per cent read Paul Biegel's answering letter;
- 85 per cent read the booklet containing tips and ideas for writing letters;
- 58 per cent used the booklet to help them write letters;
- 46 per cent wrote to two or all three of the other participants whose addresses they'd been sent.

All participants said they'd continue to write letters to friends in the future.

Agency: Responsable Communicatie/Projektmanagement

COMMENT

This was a very successful promotion, reflecting credit on the agency and its client, Dutch PTT Post.

Just telling children that letter writing is easy and fun, was unlikely to work. What did work was exciting their imaginations, equipping them physically with what they needed to start writing and providing them with previously unknown friends to write to. Expert help was enlisted, from a successful children's author and from an editorial panel, to help create the library kit, and schools and public libraries were enrolled both to disseminate the scheme and to strengthen the learning effect. Great care was taken in every detail of the execution: even a special computer program was developed to match up children with their pen pals. Relevant and appealing rewards were offered to children participating.

Responsable make the point that children respond well to a promotion that 'takes them seriously' – they reject promotions that treat them casually.

Goodyear is Looking for Winners

Goodyear Sucht Sieger

Background

In Germany Goodyear has a chain of tyre and car service centres. Some are owned and managed by Goodyear, others are operated by franchise partners.

Existing users of these Goodyear centres express a high degree of satisfaction with the service they receive. However, the centres were not widely known and in early 1990 they were not operating at full capacity.

More German motorists needed to be induced to try their service.

The Promotion

During the period 10–31 May 1990 (12 working days) Goodyear announced it was 'Looking for Winners' (*'Goodyear Sucht Sieger'*).

Existing customers visiting 100 Goodyear Tyre and Service Centres in the western part of Germany, plus other interested motorists, were invited to complete a promotional card with both their own name and address and car details, *and those of a friend too.* By doing so they qualified for instant-win prizes of, for example, pocket calculators and ballpoint pens.

Then they were entered in a nationwide draw in which first prizes were weekends in Milan, to include a visit to the opera at La Scala, a shopping expedition and VIP attendance at the Monza Formula 1 race, with a visit to the Goodyear pit-stop. This Milan trip was for two couples: the motorist who had filled in the card and the friend whose details he had written on the card – both accompanied by their spouses or other guests.

All friends named on all cards received a card from Goodyear inviting them to visit the centre, bringing in their car for a valuable three-point check, free.

The promotion was announced to the motoring public by stickers on all bills and correspondence etc from the centres in the period leading up to 10 May; by approximately 40,000 personalized letters to existing

GOODYEAR
Freundschaftsaktion vom 10.5.–31.5.90

sucht SIEGER

Gewinnen Sie...
ein Traumwochenende
für 2 x 2 Personen
mit Shopping und
Scala in Mailand,
heißen Motoren und
Boxenbesuch beim
Grand-Prix der
Formel 1 in Monza.

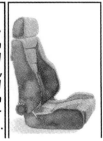

'Goodyear is looking for Winners'

clients from centre managers; by posters and other display materials in and outside the centres; and by promotional badges worn by all staff.

To motivate staff mystery shoppers called on all outlets and the centre recruiting the largest number of new clients won a trip to Monza, with spouse.

Results

Turnover in the participating outlets increased by an average of approximately 25 per cent during the promotion.

The winning centre recruited 457 new clients as a result of the promotion.

Prompted awareness of Goodyear Tyre and Car Service rose from 12.5 per cent before the promotion to 30.5 per cent afterwards.

Goodyear obtained valuable addresses of potential new customers.

Agency: Frey/Beaumont Bennett

COMMENT

This is a good example of how existing customers can be excellent recruiters of new customers.

AOSEPT NATIONAL LENS-CARE CONSULTATION WEEKS

AOSEPT NATIONALE KONTAKTLINSEN-PFLEGE BERATUNGSWOCHEN

BACKGROUND

Aosept is a revolutionary product for contact lenses, a one-step, preservative-free, disinfecting and neutralizing system. At the time of its launch in Germany in 1989, competitors' lens cleaners were two-step products, requiring both a disinfectant and a neutralizing solution. Aosept, by contrast, needed only a single solution to do both jobs, making it much easier and more convenient to use, and offering a useful price advantage of between 5 to 10 per cent.

Given these significant product pluses, Ciba Geigy backed the German launch, through its Ciba Vision division, with the usual advertising support.

However, initial sales failed to live up to expectations and a subsequent review revealed a number of related problems.

Crucial to the success of such a product is the confident support of opticians. Opticians have an almost doctor–patient relationship with their customers: they 'prescribe' lens-care products and are very aware of their responsibilities. They are unlikely to propose a change of brand to their existing customers without a strong reason for doing so, and post-launch research indicated they lacked the necessary confidence in Aosept to recommend such a change. They still had reservations about the whole concept of a one-step lens cleaner, and these reservations were being strongly reinforced by a barrage of critical comments from competitors' sales forces. Meanwhile, the majority of contact lens wearers hesitated to switch to a new brand of cleaner unless it was on the recommendation of their optician, or at least with their optician's approval.

These trade and sales force problems were addressed first. A seminar on Aosept was mounted for Ciba Vision sales personnel and they were equipped with new and powerful presentation aids. A programme of mailings backed up the sales force's communication of Aosept's merits to opticians.

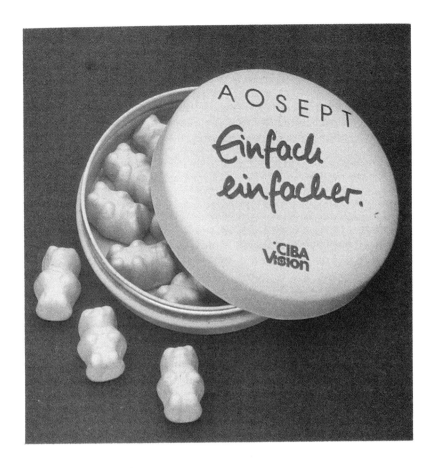

Aosept invited wearers of contact lenses to attend consultations

THE CONSUMER PROGRAMME

Everything was now in place for a renewed attack on the consumer.

An eight-week campaign in 1990, using tip-in cards in magazines and radio announcements, invited contact lens wearers to attend a consultation with their opticians during 'National Lens-Care Consultation Weeks'.

Aosept test sets were provided free to opticians agreeing to participate, equipping them with the means to demonstrate the brand's one-step convenience to their customers.

Results

Of the approximately 6000 opticians in Germany, approximately 1000 were targeted to participate in National Lens-Care Consultation Weeks. In practice 1600 did so.

Sales of Aosept rose sharply during both the sales force/trade and consumer phases, and have now plateaued out at more than 500 per cent higher than before this campaign.

Agency: Cato Johnson

COMMENT

'Media' used to promote sales are almost as varied as advertising media, and their careful and effective selection is just as important. This selection is not just a question of minimizing costs, but also of providing an appropriate and supportive context for the promotion – what in advertising would be called an appropriate 'editorial' context. Thus, Scouts and Cubs were perfect recruiting agents as shoe-shine boys for Johnson Wax's One-Step, as were retired employees of Netherlands Railways for the Senior Citizens' Rail Card, and satisfied customers for Goodyear Tyre and Service Centres.

Ciba Vision and Cato Johnson successfully identified opticians as the most powerful demonstrators of Aosept's benefits, the appropriate environment in which to allow the target consumer to try the brand.

HALF-PRICE SPRITE

1/2 PRIS SPRITE

BACKGROUND

To launch Sprite successfully in Denmark was always going to be a big challenge because lemon and lime drinks, similar to Sprite, were already offered by 7Up, Faxe Kondi and other smaller brands, which already held approximately 15 per cent of the Danish soft drink market. Sprite as a brand name was effectively unknown to 13 to 29 year olds, who formed the key target market. Retailers were not going to be overjoyed at the idea they should have to find shelf space for yet another soft drink. And to justify keeping space on the shelves Sprite was going to have to sell through briskly to the consumer.

The key task was to get young Danes trying Sprite quickly.

THE PROMOTION

The official launch date was 1 November 1988 and was celebrated by the release in Copenhagen of helium balloons in the form of Sprite bottles 4 metres high.

A week before, local press advertisements pictured Sprite and invited readers to 'Guess what new soft drink is coming to town ... and write us a slogan'. A prize of DKr5000 was offered for the winning slogan, multiplied by seven if sent in straight away, ie seven days before the launch, by six if sent six days before the launch ... and so on. This was a good incentive to start thinking hard about Sprite NOW!

Most important, initial stocks of Sprite were offered at half their normal retail price – an offer of generosity unprecedented in the Danish soft drinks market. This 'trial' price was advertised on both radio and television.

'Half Price Sprite!'

Results

Eleven hundred slogans were sent in during the seven days preceding launch.

By the end of 1988 Sprite was stocked in 85 per cent of supermarkets, service stations and kiosks.

Fifty-five per cent of 13–29 year olds had tried Sprite. A further 23 per cent had heard of it.

Sprite's share of the lemon and lime sector of the soft drinks market reached 50 per cent by the end of January 1989.

Agency: Cato Johnson

COMMENT

Price discounting is all too often defensive, as a response to pressure from competitors or the distributive trade.

This promotion reminds us that when used boldly, as opposed to grudgingly, a bargain price offer can be the most aggressive of promotional techniques.

There was no question of the cheaper price cheapening Sprite's image: the surrounding promotional activities and launch advertising made quite clear that this was a substantial brand making a serious and determined bid for the Danish public's custom. The half-price offer was manifestly a dramatic invitation to try this new brand: it was very unlikely to be misinterpreted as a desperate admission that Sprite could not sustain its full price.

One Left Wellie

Background

Gaining trial can be a requirement of business-to-business selling, as well as consumer goods marketing. Here's an outstandingly successful promotion for a property development.

In 1987 Sheraton Securities International were building a new business centre at Sunbury. The development was to a high standard of construction, and the location was ideal for any business requiring close access to the facilities of central London, to the UK motorway network and to Heathrow and Gatwick airports.

None the less the 'Sunbury International Business Centre' (SIBC) faced stiff competition, both from existing developments and from numerous similar business centres under construction.

Key targets were senior personnel within leading London commercial property agents. These people play a very influential role in advising clients seeking new premises. Their time is limited, however, not least because every new development is competing for their attention and custom, quite often with astonishingly generous incentives.

It was decided to concentrate on 50 of these top commercial agents, and to devise some powerful but affordable means of inducing them to visit the Sunbury site personally, to see and experience for themselves the excellence of its facilities. This was despite the fact that construction was still in progress, and that access to it was by very muddy roads and paths.

The Promotion

On Friday 27 November 1987, a pair of attractive promotion girls visited each of the 50 target agents. They delivered to each a 'left wellie' – the left boot of a pair of upmarket Hunter wellingtons, ideal for wearing when touring a muddy construction site like the Sunbury International Business Centre.

The boot was discreetly labelled 'SIBC', but the promotion girls were deliberately *not* briefed as to what this was all about, and the recipient of the boot was therefore left scratching his head as to why anybody had sent him this boot. Certainly Hunter was the most prestigious brand of rubber boots, but what was the use of a left boot without the matching right one to go with it? Very frustrating, but very intriguing.

By Friday afternoon agents were on the phone to each other, to see if anybody else knew what this was all about.

All was revealed the next day. A full-colour double-page advertisement appeared in the magazine *Estates Gazette*, the 'bible' of commercial property agents in the UK. The advertisement listed by name all the individuals who had received the boot the previous day, and invited them to visit the Sunbury International Business Centre bringing their 'left wellie' with them. On arrival the boot would be exchanged for a *pair* of the size to fit them to wear as they toured the site. And of course they could keep them afterwards.

Results

Forty-eight of the 50 agents visited the site personally, bringing their left wellies with them.

The remaining two telephoned to ask for their pair of boots to be sent to them. They were politely refused!

In summary: 96 per cent 'trial', 100 per cent awareness.

Agency: Hook Advertising

COMMENT

It was going to be difficult for the recipient to ignore the gift of the left wellie (in practice it proved impossible!). And even those recipients who did not read the *Estates Gazette* the next day, Saturday, would hear from their colleagues on the Monday that their names were listed in an advertisement. It was flattering to be identified in this way as a key individual.

• Simon Sokel – Grant & Partners • Dick Clay – Emmitt Rathbone • Rog
Saper – Jones Lang Wootton • Charles Osborne – Leighton Goldhill • Ia
Worboys – Strutt & Parker • Will Winterson – St. Quintin • David Zair –
Pepper Angliss and Yarwood • Bob Henley – Rice Henley • Tony Rowe –
Weatherall Green & Smith • Russell Meadows – Rogers Chapman • Dav
Collins – Adlers • Martyn Elkington – Allsop & Company • Gary Diamo
– Bernard Diamond & Ptnrs. • Tony Thorpe – Bernard Thorpe & Ptnrs
• Tim Gould – Bonsor Penningtons • Vic Spencer – Brian Cooper & Co.
• Mark Potter – Bryant & Partners • David South – Chamberlain & Will
• David Weston – Chesterton • Roger Duke – Donaldsons • John Heawc
– Debenham Tewson & Chinnocks • Kevin Coles – Conway Relf • Vanes
Clarke – Clive Lewis & Partners • Edward Hawkins – Drivers Jonas
• Andy Cole – Dron & Wright • Harvey Novik – Druce & Co. • Barry Rot
– Edward Erdman • Chris Goodwin – Gooch & Wagstaff • Tim Flett –
Fletcher King • Paul Bacon – Healey & Baker • Richard Hull – Henry
Butcher & Co. • Paul Miller – Paul Miller & Co. • Paul Crowson – Mills &
Wood • Nick Epps – Matthews Goodman • Philip Strevens – King & Co.
• Paul Jenkins – Herring Son & Daw • Peter McMillan – Hillier Parker N
& Rowden • Robert Sinclair – Robert Neil & Co. • Richard Storey – Rich:
Ellis • John Kingston – Russell Cash & Co. • Jeremy Aitchison – Savills
• Fergus Kinloch – Vigers • Tim Bloomfield – Clive Lewis & Ptnrs.
• Michael Croydon – D.E.&J. Levy • Peter Bennett –
Eyles Fellows • Mike Parry – Fletcher King • Gary
Leigh – Grant & Partners • Simon Fryer – Campbell
Gordon • William Webb – Fuller Peiser • Andrew Burt –
Jones Lang Wootton • Graham Hayman – Knight Frank & Rutley…

What possible use is one wellie?

If you were one of the select few who received a green left wellington boot yesterday, then you're probably wondering where you can pick up the right one.
Easy!
All you have to do is hop down in person to Sunbury International Business Centre at Junction 1 off the M3.
You have to have a genuine S.I.B.C. wellie to qualify, so please don't take the label off!
Call Henrietta now on the S.I.B.C. hotline (Between 10am & 4pm Mon – Fri) for full directions and a convenient appointment to view – 0932 787782.

A development by

Sheraton Securities International plc

in conjunction with

ƎSⱮ

Gordon, Linch+Co
Surveyors and Valuers
10 Sedley Place, Mayfair, W1R 1HG
01·409 1441

Walker Son & Packman   01-606 8111
1–6 Trump Street,
London EC2V 8DD.

Peter Taylor & Company
16 Bolton Street, London W1Y 7PA
01·499 5511
Fax 01 491 3288

4

REPEAT PURCHASE

INTRODUCTION

Many of the brands that feature in this book need to be purchased frequently if they are to succeed commercially. OK, so the sale of a long lease on a commercial property acquits sales promotion of further responsibility for the foreseeable future in our last case studied, 'One Left Wellie', and similarly a new Range Rover won't need replacing for quite a while. But coffee, contact lens cleaners, soft drinks, household cleaners, magazines (to mention just some of the other sectors we've been studying already) are for regular, repeat consumption. And the competitive battle is won or lost by the brands' ability to win the loyalty of consumers over time, over a series of purchases.

In the final analysis this loyal repeat purchase will be achieved only by brands that deliver what consumers want, that provide the functional and psychological benefits the public is looking for. But assuming a brand is capable of delivering these benefits, sales promotional techniques can encourage consumers to make a habit of buying the brand, at least for a specified number of purchases.

Here are some examples of sales promotion doing just that.

LIGHT UP THE WORLD CUP WITH MATCHES

ACCENDI I MONDIALI CON FIAMMIFERI

BACKGROUND

Buying matches on my visits to Italy has always been a pleasure for me as a foreigner: those very typical cerini *(literally 'little wax tapers') in their tiny and often beautifully decorated boxes, and those brightly coloured books of matches.*

In fact, sales of matches in Italy were in decline in 1990. Consumer attitudes were that matches were downmarket and arguably obsolete. The range of opportunities for using matches in the home had been steadily narrowing, with the growth of electrical and other modern forms of heating and cooking. Cigarette consumption was down, and lighter manufacturers were competing especially fiercely for this sector of the market.

All types of matches were suffering, but the Italian matchmakers' association, the Consorzio Industrie Fiammiferi, agreed with their agency to make a start first on book matches, bought mainly by young adult male smokers.

The fact that, in 1990, the soccer World Cup finals were being contested in Italy was clearly too good an opportunity to miss, if these young men were to be wooed back to matches.

THE PROMOTION

From May 1990 (just before the first match of the tournament kicked off) and throughout the finals, book matches sported the strip of the 24 competing nations. Each cover carried a highly stylized design of one team's shirt and shorts, while the back of the book of matches carried brief details of the soccer achievements and prospects of that country.
    This promotion was announced in 15-second TV spots showing a blazing match and inviting viewers to 'light up the World Cup'. These spots were transmitted during television programmes which previewed each of the competing 24 teams in the run-up to the competition. Further support was provided by radio spots targeted at young adult male audiences, and advertisements in newspapers including the mass circulation *La Gazetta dello Sport*.

'Light up the World Cup!' – with these book matches

Results

During the World Cup months of June and July sales of book matches soared by 23 per cent.

Agency: Cato Johnson

COMMENT

Marshall McLuhan pointed out that the 'media is the message'.

'Light up the World Cup' illustrates that 'the packaging can be the promotion'.

Packaging isn't limited only to *announcing* a promotional offer – it can be given a promotional value itself.

RUDDLES'S TUPPENCE HA'PENNY PINT

BACKGROUND

Ruddles bitter beer is a successful example of a large British brewing concern, Grand Metropolitan Brewing, distributing a regional beer on a wide, national scale, while still preserving its traditional character. Ruddles brings to this wider market a reputation for quality, strength and taste – 'small independent brewer' values.

The brand faces price cutting from some competitive beers, but as Ruddles has been actively establishing a premium price for itself, it has held back from responding in kind. None the less the brand needed a way of rewarding loyal Ruddles drinkers with some close alternative to competitors' price cuts, compatible with Ruddles's premium positioning.

THE PROMOTION

Ruddles drinkers were offered a pint for the price of a pint of beer in 1912: 'tuppence ha'penny', ie two and a half old pennies.

They collected one old halfpenny with each pint of Ruddles they bought. Five 'ha'pennies' could then be used to 'buy' the next pint.

The halfpennies were genuine, ie they were the coins which had been withdrawn from circulation in the early 1970s when the British currency was decimalized.

The promotion was offered to selected pubs (both 'tied' outlets owned by the brewer, and 'free trade' pubs and clubs) in the last quarter of 1989.

In participating pubs the promotion was announced on drip mats and on posters which illustrated objects from 1912 such as a clock, a watch and a *Times* newspaper of the period.

Beer at 1912 prices!

Results

All 'tied' outlets offered the promotion participated. Eighty per cent of the 'free trade' pubs and clubs offered the promotion also participated (a 30 per cent better take-up than had been achieved by earlier Ruddles promotions).

Promotional sales targets were achieved by the end of the first week of the four-week promotional selling period.

After the promotion sales in participating outlets continued into 1990 at levels typically 10 per cent above pre-promotion levels.

Trade and sales force enthusiasm for the promotion led to it being run in a further 1800 pubs and clubs in 1990.

Agency: Dean Street Marketing

COMMENT

A simplistic, mechanistic description of this promotion would be that it offered 'Buy Five Pints, Get One Free', using 'tokens' as proofs of purchase.

These mechanics were transformed, however, by the play of creative imagination on these bits and pieces of promotional technique. The chance to buy a pint of Ruddles for only tuppence ha'penny was much more attention grabbing and intriguing than a 'Buy Five, Get One Free' headline. The real old halfpennies were interesting objects in their own right, fascinating to handle and examine closely. Some of the younger drinkers would have been too young at the time they were withdrawn from circulation to remember them. Older drinkers were no doubt delighted to explain them – they were a good talking point – putting Ruddles firmly into pub conversations. Who is this king on the coin? (George V.) How many old pennies were there in a new penny? (2.4.) What does this 'Ind Imp' stand for round the edge of the coin? (Emperor of India.) Also, the fact that these were the actual copper coins, five of them, that would have bought a pint in 1912 made this almost more of a celebration of Ruddles's heritage than a price promotion.

WIN A GREAT DAY OUT AT WALLABY PARK
GAGNE UNE JOURNÉE DE FÊTE A WALIBI

BACKGROUND

During the cold, wet Belgian winters, grocers' shelves and shoppers' food baskets are piled high with bananas, one of the few fresh fruits to be found then, and a favourite with young children.

Come summer, however, locally grown fruits are in season, and bananas get pushed to the back of shoppers' minds and to the back of grocers' displays.

There's no question of bananas not being in free supply: bananas are mostly imported into Belgium from tropical countries where bananas are produced all the year round. It's simply a question of Belgians not being in the habit of eating as many bananas in the summer as in the winter. At least not until Chiquita, Belgium's largest banana importer (with a 60–70 per cent market share), decided to run a promotion in 1989 to do something about changing this habit.

Three groups needed influencing in favour of bananas: children, who are the main consumers; mothers who buy bananas for their children, especially if their children ask for them; retailers who need to carry adequate stocks of bananas and to display them for sale where they can be seen, if bananas are to stand any chance of competing fairly with other fruits as they come into season.

THE PROMOTION

Children were invited to 'Win a Great Day Out at Wallaby Park', Belgium's leading amusement location, for the whole family (four people). To compete children were required either to draw a picture or write a sentence linking a wallaby with a Chiquita banana. Their mothers were required to validate their entries by enclosing proofs of purchase of 4 kilos of Chiquita bananas (a promotional sticker was issued by cashiers with each kilo bought).

Four kilos represented an average family's *wintertime* consumption of bananas – therefore a transformation of their summer eating habits.

The promotion was announced on leaflets at the point of purchase and by a television commercial which gained extra attention by being the

'Win a Great Day Out' with Chiquita Bananas

first to run on both the French language and the recently deregulated Flemish channels.

Further exposure was given to Chiquita bananas, and the Wallaby Park promotion, by a series of beach games which Chiquita organized along the Belgian coast. Coupons redeemable against a kilo of Chiquita bananas were awarded to winners, adding to the proofs of purchase required to enter the Wallaby Park competition.

Retailers were involved too. In each box of bananas a lottery ticket gave grocers a chance to win a visit to the Chiquita day out at Wallaby Park as one of 50 VIPs, bringing their families with them, of course. On the day a further draw awarded prizes such as video cameras and stereo equipment to 16 of them. By placing the means of entering this trade promotion in all boxes *all* banana retailers were involved – not just the larger grocers at whom so much promotional activity is targeted.

Two hundred and fifty wholesalers were also invited, with their families.

Results

Children entered the competition in their thousands.

More than 60,000 entries were received for the trade promotion – a huge number in relation to the scale of the Belgian market (very approximately 14,000 outlets for bananas). Small retailers were vigorous participants.

Chiquita sales increased by 60,000 boxes (each of 18 kilos) in summer 1989, compared with the previous year, almost eliminating the usual summertime dip.

Along the Belgian coast Chiquita's market share advanced to 80 per cent.

Six thousand family groups of four arrived at Wallaby Park for the 'Chiquita Banana Day' on 8 October.

Agency: Cato Johnson

COMMENT

This was a straightforward but relevant prize promotion, turned into a big success by hard-working exploitation through a number of inter-related channels: point of purchase; holiday beaches; television.

HEINZ 100 DAY DRIVEAWAY

BACKGROUND

HJ Heinz is one of the UK's most successful food manufacturers, with brand leadership in a number of sectors such as soups, beans, pasta products, puddings, baby foods, ketchup etc.

'Heinz' is similarly one of the UK's strongest brand names, supporting and justifying a premium price over retailers' own-label versions of these foods.

This envied position has been won and maintained only by vigorously supporting first-class products with a long series of famous advertising campaigns. And, more recently in history, by mounting large-scale national sales promotions across a range of 'core' Heinz products every autumn/winter.

The aim of these annual promotional pushes typically has been to encourage an increased rate of sale for Heinz products to consumers, via dominant displays at the point of purchase. Stimulating multiple repeat purchase across the Heinz range, by providing an extra reason why Heinz varieties should be purchased in preference to competitors' and retailers' own-label offerings. These were once again the objectives of the promotion which ran from September to December 1990, and which built on and represented the pinnacle of this earlier activity.

THE PROMOTION

The 'Heinz 100 Day Driveaway' offered a prize of a car to be won every day throughout this three-month period.

The car was the popular Metro, in a limited edition of 'Metro 57s'. The number '57' is indissolubly linked with Heinz branding in the British public's mind.

The Metro 57s carried discreet '57' branding on their side doors, sun roof and wheel trims, but more strikingly each had a personalized registration number plate. Negotiation with the British vehicle licensing authority limited the issue of a 'H 57' prefix to these 100 cars, and allowed winners to complete the remaining three letters of the registration with

Over 11 million entries were received for this Heinz '100 Day Driveaway'

their own three initials. Extras such as fog lamps, central locking, stereo radio/cassette and alarm completed the appeal of these unique prizes.

Other prizes, also 'branded' to Heinz, were awarded daily too: 57 Heinz/ Automobile Association road atlases of Britain; and 100 vouchers, each redeemable against purchases of Heinz products worth £5.70.

To compete for these prizes consumers were required simply to write their names and addresses on the back of any promotional or standard Heinz label, or on plain paper, mailing it to the address stated on all promotional announcements.

There was no limit on the number of entries made, but only one entry on plain paper was accepted in each envelope.

All entries were put into a daily draw to determine winners.

The promotion was announced to consumers on the labels of 80 million promotional cans of Heinz baked beans, spaghetti products, tomato and other ready-to-serve soup varieties and treacle sponge pudding.

National and regional newspapers carried advertisements for the promotion.

A whole series of 'tailored' versions of this national promotion were created for leading UK grocery chains, to help 'clinch' negotiations for large displays in their stores.

Results

Large off-shelf displays were achieved in key accounts.

Over 11 million labels were mailed in as entries, nearly doubling the number of entries to any of the previous schemes.

On average seven labels were sent in by each participant. Approximately one and a half million consumers entered.

Research indicated that a significant number of consumers who entered changed their normal purchasing behaviour in order to do so.

Many of them increased their pantry stocks with Heinz products, tried a new Heinz variety or switched to Heinz from a competitive brand which they normally bought.

Agency: Clarke Hooper

COMMENT

The 'classic' sales promotional technique to generate repeat purchase is to require the consumer to *collect* a number of proofs of purchase. This technique is illustrated by the two preceeding studies of Ruddles beer and Chiquita bananas promotions.

The 'Heinz 100 Day Driveaway' illustrates a different approach. Each purchase qualifies the consumer to participate in the promotion immediately (and immediacy is an attractive feature of any promotion). However, multiple entries are encouraged by multiplying the opportunities to gain rewards (in this case *daily* prizes, over an extended period).

It's a different approach that succeeded: a huge number of consumers sent in, on average, seven proofs of purchase.

AIR MILES

BACKGROUND

All airlines have empty seats on certain flights to certain destinations at certain times of the year. In 1988 this was true even of British Airways, one of the world's most successful and profitable airlines.

Filling some of these seats, even at deeply discounted prices, would clearly boost the marginal profitability of unfilled flights. However, targeting the audience for such discounts posed serious problems: they were all too likely to be taken up by the airline's existing customers, diluting rather than increasing revenue. What was needed was a new market for these unfilled seats.

The breakthrough (as so often in innovative marketing) was to stop worrying about unsold seats as a problem and see them as an opportunity instead. It would be an opportunity to use them as the rewards for loyal repeat-purchase of other companies' products and services, rewards which these other companies would be willing to pay for.

THE AIR MILES SCHEME

The 'Air Miles' scheme was launched on 1 November 1988.

Participating companies/brands offer their customers Air Miles vouchers, typically at the point of purchase.

For example, in the early days of the scheme the following was done.

- Shell offered 1 Air Mile for every £6 worth of petrol purchased
- The National Westminster Bank offered initially one Air Mile for every £10 spent on NatWest Access cards. Subsequently, customers could earn 200 Air Miles for taking out a NatWest Visa card and then 1 Air Mile for every £10 spent on it.
- The Burton Group made vigorous use of Air Miles for a series of continuous but changing tactical offers, from most companies in the group (Principles, Debenhams, Dorothy Perkins, Champion Sport etc). For example, they offered 500 Air Miles when £75 was spent on tennis equipment at Champion Sport; 500 Air Miles when £100 was spent in Principles.

One Air Mile entitles the holder to a mile of free travel with British Airways. Consumers are encouraged to register as collectors (via

Over three million people registered as collectors of Air Miles in the first four years of the scheme

advertisements in the press and leaflets issued with the Air Miles vouchers). They then receive full details of the world-wide destinations accessible using Air Miles, details of flights and the number of Air Miles required to reach each destination from the various UK airports from which British Airways operates.

Other companies/brands issuing Air Miles are also listed in this package sent to consumers. As each participant is granted exclusivity in its product/service sector for 12 months, it clearly benefits all participants for their consumers to know they can accelerate qualifying for a free flight by collecting vouchers from elsewhere too. In 1991, for example, Air Miles were offered by the following companies to their consumers in Britain and/or Northern Ireland.

Alfred Marks Bureau	Guinness
Andras House	Hertz UK
Automobile Association	Invergordon Distillers
BDG Group	John Lunne Jewellers
Black & Decker	National Westminster Bank
British Airways	PGL Adventure Holidays
British Car Parks	Pre-Flight Travel

Bullrush Peat	Shell NI
Caledonian Airways	Shell UK
Comet	Spillers Foods
Coutts/Ulster Bank	Sun Alliance
Dale Farm	T&F Inns
Decco NI	Tayto NI
Dolmio (Mars Foods)	Thomas Cook Direct
ESD Video	Welcome Break
General Accident	

Air Miles were also used in business-to-business promotion by the following.

ADT Security	MK Electric
Air Call	MTV
Arthur Bell	NEC
Creda	Newey & Eyre
CPC	Newman Distributors
Drayton Controls	Osram
Encyclopaedia Britannica	Pyrene
Ericsson	Redring Electric
Esso Petroleum	Silentnight
Fichemaster	Sinclair Opticals
H Morris & Co Furniture	Spectrum Marketing
Harris Distribution	Spillers Foods
Hewlett Packard	Toolrange
Hickson	Toshiba
IBM	Waddingtons
Kraft General Foods	WW Hawes
Lexmark	Wiggins Teape Fine Papers
Mars Confectionery	

And, finally, Air Miles were used in 1991 in employee motivation programmes by the following.

Allied Dunbar	IBM
DEC	Pallas Leasing
Ford	Total Oil
Forte	Vauxhall

Once collectors have the necessary number of Air Miles for their chosen destination they simply cash in their vouchers for flights through approved travel agents, or by phoning an Air Miles reservation centre direct.

As British Airways had carefully collated and analysed data on unused capacity for over a decade, the airline was able to allocate seats to a new Air Miles class, on many of their flights to 152 world-wide destinations. Air Miles travellers enjoy all the in-flight benefits and services of other passengers, but as is common with other 'promotional' tickets (eg Apex), the flights cannot be transferred or refunded once booked.

First-time fliers with Air Miles are offered a 5 per cent discount: ie 5 per cent fewer Air Miles are required to qualify for their flights.

Children aged below 12 years require only 75 per cent of the Air Miles listed for each destination, and infants of 2 years and under, not occupying a seat, only 10 per cent.

Here are two real examples of members of the public joining the scheme soon after its inception and collecting and using their Air Miles. Only the names have been changed.

Mr Smith registered in December 1988
He collected:
    50 Air Miles as a starter bonus
    80 from Natwest
   200 from Shell
   410 from the Burton Group
   <u>260 from Texas Homecare</u>
1,000 Air Miles in Total

In July 1989 Mr Smith booked two return flights to Amsterdam.

Mr Jones registered in January 1989
He collected:
    50 Air Miles as a starter bonus
    35 from Natwest
    70 from Shell
  100 from the Automobile Association
  250 from Allied Carpets
   55 from Texas Homecare
  300 from the Rover Group
   <u>40 from the *Daily Express*</u>
 900 Air Miles in Total

In July 1989 Mr Jones booked two return flights to Paris.

DEVELOPMENTS AND SPIN-OFFS

Air Miles is now an established part of the UK promotional scene, with high levels of consumer awareness.

In the financial year 1991/2, approximately 170,000 flights were booked with Air Miles.

Over three million consumers have now registered as collectors, a valuable database which Air Miles Travel Promotions are making available to other clients under strictly controlled conditions.

Sub-brands have also been developed, for example, Air Miles 'Latitudes', launched in March 1991, targets frequent travellers.

'Smart' cards are due to replace paper vouchers soon, in some areas of operation.

COMMENT

Promotional schemes to encourage and reward long-term loyalty to a brand have been around in the UK since at least the middle 19th century, when the Co-op started offering shoppers a dividend payable on all purchases at the end of the trading year.

More recently, cigarette and oil companies have run long-term schemes in which vouchers issued with each purchase are redeemable against merchandise listed in promotional catalogues. In the 1960s and 1970s trading stamps were all the rage, with Green Shield Stamps in particular being offered in many grocery stores, on petrol forecourts and in many other sectors too.

Air Miles follow this tradition. Like trading stamps they gain in appeal by being available from different sources, with different purchases, but with the important plus point for companies participating that each is granted exclusivity in its sector. The rewards offered are much narrower in scope than those available from trading stamps, but arguably travel now plays the role in many consumers' aspirations that, in the 1960s and 1970s, was played by the household appliances which then filled the pages of the stamp and voucher catalogues.

A strong plus point of the scheme, in communication terms, is the direct link with reality of Air Miles, ie the fact that an Air Mile collected means another *real* mile the collector has qualified to fly. Too many loyalty-building schemes deal in 'points' or 'tokens', which give the target audience little feel for the physical reality of what they can earn with them.

Who said that sales promotion was necessarily 'tactical' and 'short term', by the way? How many advertising campaigns that started in November 1988 are still running today?

5

BRAND IMAGE

INTRODUCTION

It was in the middle 1950s that sales promotion began to assume its present importance across Europe. It was then that supply began to outstrip demand in one sector after another, as industries were rebuilt after wartime devastation, and sellers' markets became highly competitive buyers' markets instead.

The consensus at that time, in even very sophisticated marketing circles, was that sales promotion was essentially a *tactical* weapon, concerned with winning this month's battles rather than long-term wars. Advertising, product development, packaging – these were seen as the strategic elements in marketing a brand, the tools to be deployed to win permanent advantage over competitors. The 'brand image' was what counted in the medium to longer term, and sales promotion was regarded as something that took place out there in the hustle and bustle of the market place, somehow separate from these brand image-building marketing activities.

By the early 1970s a number of practitioners and writers (the present author included) were questioning this negative and dismissive attitude to sales promotion. Why should a sales promotion offer appearing on the back of a pack be less important in influencing consumers' view of what's inside the pack than a television commercial for the brand? How are consumers to know that the TV message is 'important', but the back-of-pack promotional message is 'unimportant'. What makes the front of the pack so influential in shaping attitudes to the brand that large fees are paid to leading designers to get it right, whereas the assistant brand manager is allowed to cover the back with whatever promotion he's come up with for the sales force this month?

Over the past two decades any remaining scepticism about the likelihood of consumer attitudes being influenced by sales promotional activities has been largely overwhelmed by the weight and all pervasiveness of sales promotion, in many European markets. It becomes very difficult to believe that *only* the advertising of a brand is shaping the public's opinion of it, if in practice more money is being spent on other forms of marketing support for the brand, notably sales promotion. It becomes *necessary* for sales promotion to help strengthen the brand image.

Here are some examples of promotion working hard to do so.

CITIZENS! LET OUR TICKETS UNITE US
CITOYENS, UNISSONS NOS TICKETS
BACKGROUND

Throughout France 1989 was celebrated as the bicentenary of the French Revolution, the celebrations coming to a grand climax on Bastille Day, 14 July.

In Paris 14 July was marked by the traditional grand parade down the Champs Elysées, by a series of spectacular events throughout the city, and as always by fireworks and dancing in the streets at the end of the day.

The Parisian public transport system – buses, underground and urban trains – played its part by offering free travel to all passengers on 14 July. And, in words echoing those of La Marseillaise, *by exhorting fellow citizens to join together and unite:* 'Citoyens! Unissons', *in the following promotion.*

CITOYENS! UNISSONS NOS TICKETS

DES MILLIERS DE SACS A DOS A GAGNER

POUR JOUER, GRATTEZ! Et découvrez l'un des 4 personnages clés de la révolution: DANTON, LA FAYETTE, LOUIS XVI ou ROBESPIERRE. TROUVEZ parmi les voyageurs les détenteurs des 3 autres personnages et constituez l'un des 1789 GROUPES GAGNANTS. UNISSEZ VOS TICKETS et rendez-vous ensemble au stand d'accueil de l'un des 14 points clés. Vous recevrez chacun un superbe sac à dos... révolutionnaire!

Grattez
et ▶
révélez

LA FAYETTE

votre Identité Révolutionnaire

LES 14 POINTS CLES DU 14 JUILLET

'Citizens! Let Our Tickets Unite Us' – a 'revolutionary' promotion for public transport in Paris

THE PROMOTION

Early on the morning of 14 July 'Welcome Stands' were set up at 14 key points on the public transport network in central Paris: Notre Dame; Gare de Lyon; Opéra etc.

By 10 o'clock in the morning everything was ready to go: from then until 5 o'clock in the afternoon, the 200 staff manning these stands handed out free scratch cards (*'tickets à gratter'*) to passengers.

Each card, when scratched, revealed the face of one or other of four leading characters of the Revolution: Louis XVI; Robespierre; La Fayette; or Danton.

Passengers were encouraged to show the faces on their cards to other passengers, to see if a set of all four faces could be made up. If so, then the four passengers presented their cards, together, at one of the 14 stands by 6.00 pm (and don't forget that travel round the network was free all day), to claim their instant prize of an attractive back-pack for each, suitably decorated in the livery colours of the transport network.

Passengers failing to team up with other passengers in this way none the less had a chance to join back-pack winners in a lottery by simply writing their name and address on the back of their scratch cards and dropping them in the 'urns' provided at the 14 locations. The prizes they could win kept to the theme of the 1789 Revolution:

1   trip for two, for 12 days, in the United States, following La Fayette's footsteps in Virginia;

7   'sentences of exile', for two, in Vienna ... with a guarantee of being brought back after a weekend away, however;

8   weekends for two of 'Rêv'évolution' (the evolution of a dream!) in the Hautes Pyrénées

9   prizes of 1789 day-tickets on the Paris public transport network.

Public transport is itself an important advertising medium, and not surprisingly therefore Parisians were prepared for this package of promotional offers during the week leading up to 14 July by posters in underground stations, on bus sides, and on a special issue of bus, underground and railway maps.

Results

On the day 1.3 million cards were handed out.

Visual observation indicated that all of them were scratched.

Back-packs were awarded to all members of 1789 (!) teams of four matching faces.

A total of 98,250 scratch cards (13.23 per cent of those issued), completed with names and addresses, were dropped into the urns as entries for the lottery, to win the other one, seven, eight and nine prizes on offer.

Agency: Marco Polo

COMMENT

This was a good-humoured demonstration to the Parisian public that *their* transport system was right in there at the heart of any event in the city.

Only monarchists and sourpusses could fail to approve of this splendid promotion. The transport system, that for many Parisians is associated primarily with going to and from work, really shows its ability to enter into the spirit of a big celebration. Surely after this you'd forgive the train for being a few minutes late?!

From the banner headline down to the small print the promotion keeps its attention focused steadily on the theme of the 1789 Revolution. It's all done with great panache and confidence. To the 'liberty' to travel the network for free is added the 'fraternity' of talking to fellow passengers to compare the faces on the cards, with a total 'equality' of opportunity to win the prizes on offer.

'Vive la France!' – 'long live sales promotion of this quality'!

Bearing Gifts for any Occasion

Background

All forms of communication using paper and ink have come under competitive pressure from electronic methods. Radio and television compete with books, newspapers and magazines. Direct money transfer systems compete with cheques. The telephone and fax offer competitive alternatives to letters.

For social purposes telephoning is certainly easier and quicker than writing a letter. A letter none the less continues to have an emotional value over and above that of a telephone call. Sending a letter shows a little extra effort has been made, a little more care taken. The message communicated is in a permanent form: it can be read and read again later, each time giving pleasure. It can, if the content is appropriate, be shown by the recipient to a friend or relation. It can be kept and treasured. And – unlike the telephone – a letter does not have to limit itself only to words: a small gift can be enclosed to reinforce the emotional value of the communication.

This case study shows the Royal Mail in Britain vigorously communicating these emotional benefits, and the physical advantages of sending letters to friends and loved ones – and using a sales promotion to do so.

The Promotion

Under the headline 'Bearing Gifts for Every Occasion', the British public were offered the opportunity to send a miniature bear to a friend or loved one with an accompanying handwritten message.

Consumers were given a selection of five bears:

- bear with a heart;
- bear with champagne bottle;
- bear with a bouquet of flowers;
- bear posting a letter;
- bear with birthday cake.

With the exception of the 'birthday cake' the bears were designed to be adaptable to a range of different mailing messages. For example the 'flower' bear could be sent for 'Get well soon', 'Thank you', 'Happy Mothers' Day' etc. In addition, by offering five bears, consumers were encouraged to collect the set, either to mail out or to keep themselves.

BEARING GIFTS
FOR ANY OCCASION

Bears shown are 5% bigger than actual size.

Bears help the British Post Office promote social letter writing

The offer was announced on poster displays and on promotional leaflets in post offices, sub-post offices and other outlets retailing stamp books. Suggested messages were highlighted on the front of the leaflet to stimulate consumer mailing ideas.

The sender completed a promotional leaflet with his own and his chosen recipient's name and address, ticked which of the five bears was to be sent and wrote a message on the 'gift tag' which formed part of the application form. The leaflet was then sent in, enclosing either one cover and four stamps, or two covers and two stamps, from books of ten first-class stamps. These proof of purchase and payment requirements discreetly nudged the sender towards using first class rather than second-class mail for social purposes.

The Post Office and their agency took it from there, enclosing the selected bear and the handwritten message in a gift box, and mailing it promptly to the nominated friend or loved one.

The offer stayed open for the three month-period, April–June 1990.

Results

Over 93,000 applications for bears were received and despatched. This represented approximately 2.4 per cent of the 3.9 million application forms made available at the point of purchase – a very high redemption for a paid-for mail-in offer announced only on posters and leaflets at the point of purchase.

The promotion was repeated in 1991 with six new bear designs, and again over 90,000 applications were received, despite a shorter promotional period.

Agency: Communicator

COMMENT

This was a very classic use of sales promotion to involve the target market in doing what the promoter would like them to do, by providing the physical means for them to do it – rather than merely talking to them about it, which is what advertising does.

Bears, especially 'teddy' bears, are irresistible when it comes to communicating sentiment and emotional warmth. Sales promotion provides the opportunity to put them into the target market's hands – not just to picture them in an advertisement.

With this promotion the Royal Mail achieved two participants for the 'price' of one: the sender and the recipient of the bear were both exposed to this evidence of the superior emotional content of a mailing rather than a telephone call. In this sense a potential of over 186,000 (rather than over 93,000) members of the public participated.

RAMADA DUCK IN A BOX

BACKGROUND

The Ramada Renaissance Hotel opened in Manchester, England, in 1988. Converted from an office block, the hotel offers a high standard of accommodation for businesspeople visiting Manchester. However, it faced stiff competition from at least five rival hotels in the city, all offering similar accommodation, and all well established.

By every means possible the Ramada Renaissance needed to get itself known and quickly to gain a reputation for warmth and that little extra friendliness that makes such an important difference for businesspeople working away from home.

The friendliness of the staff was clearly of prime importance, and this was assured by careful recruitment and training. A motto was adopted for the hotel: 'If it makes the guest smile it's done its job'. Every effort was made to make the guest feel 'at home', to avoid the impersonal anonymity of so many business hotels, to lighten guests' working days with a touch of humour.

All these efforts suddenly started to 'gel' with the introduction of a most unusual sales promotion.

THE PROMOTION

A plastic duck was placed in every bathroom before the guest's arrival. The duck was bright yellow with a red beak. In fact, it was a child's duck, designed to float round the bath and keep the child amused while Mum soaped its ears and shampooed its hair.

But for an adult businessman – or woman?!

Why not? After a hard day's work in a strange city what better way to relax than to lie soaking in your bath in the Renaissance, nudging Reggie (that was the duck's name) round with your toe, steering him between your knees, and – if it had been that bad a day – telling him how awful everybody had been at the meeting.

A small tent card in every room explained further:

GOOD HOME WANTED !

How can you resist him?

In your bathroom you will find Reggie, our very own and very special duck. You can take him home to bathe with and to look after - *with our compliments.*

But if you know of anyone else who can give a good home to one of Reggie's feathered friends - Reception will be only too pleased to mail one in a special crate, anywhere in the United Kingdom* for only £2.50.

RAMADA®

* For overseas addresses please contact Reception.

Reggie the Ramada duck

The 'special crate' followed through this humorous approach. Made of stout, corrugated board, it was printed to look like wood planking and marked:

Almost
LIVESTOCK
WITH CARE

The address label on the 'crate' was headed:

DUCK IN A BOX
On Migration to ...

and, after the address:

From
RAMADA

Results

The promotion ran initially for four months, April–July 1989, and by the end of this period the Renaissance Hotel was fully booked throughout the week. Undoubtedly the duck contributed to this success.

Reggie rapidly became famous, initially by word-of-mouth. Hearing about him on their boss's return secretaries started adding the Ramada to their list of Manchester hotels. New guests checked into the Renaissance seeking reassurance that they'd find the duck in their bathroom. They would: as the promotion made a profit (the surplus from mailing ducks to friends and relations exceeding the cost of free Reggies), the scheme was extended indefinitely.

Word-of-mouth publicity was boosted by exceptional coverage of Reggie in TV programmes in Britain, continental Europe and even Australasia, and in newspaper articles in many countries.

Reggie became the 'star' of the Renaissance Hotel's Christmas card in 1989, and appeared on all the hotel's literature.

Other Ramada hotels adopted the 'Duck in a Box'.

Agency: Colin Jarvis

COMMENT

This was a great promotional concept, because it was bold, original and *relevantly* 'zany'.

If Ramada management gave the go-ahead to this idea, they must be entertaining people. I'll stay with them next time!

DMC OFFERS YOU THIS DRESS PATTERN – SPECIALLY COMMISSIONED FROM A YOUNG PARIS DESIGNER

DMC VOUS OFFRE LE PATRON D'UN JEUNE CRÉATEUR PARISIEN

BACKGROUND

'Tous Textiles' was launched in France by DMC in 1987. This is a thread of man-made fibre, in a range of colours, sold originally in 100-metre reels, and – as its name implies – suitable for sewing all types of fabric.

DMC's reputation among women who make some of their own clothes was primarily as a producer of embroidery floss. In the sewing thread sector DMC faced stiff competition, notably from a well-established brand leader, Gutermann. 'Tous Textiles' none the less made good progress, and a decision was taken to extend the brand into 200, 500 and 1000-metre reels in 1989.

The brand was supported by an advertising campaign, but sewing threads are purchased quite infrequently: the average sales of this type of thread is around 100 reels per month in each of approximately 2000 outlets.

An additional positive message needed to be communicated at the point of purchase, to be sure of reaching French dressmakers, when they were sufficiently interested in the idea of making something new for themselves to have gone shopping for ideas and materials.

Young women were the prime target market: less set in their ways than older women and offering rich, long-term sales potential to a brand that could make its mark with them now.

THE PROMOTION

DMC commissioned a dress design from Franck Joseph Bastille. This young Parisian designer, as the point of purchase displays put it,

has already had the media enthusing about his work in a big way. A member of the youthfully talented Groupe des Halles he's rapidly been spotted by all the leading fashion editors. Subtly interlacing traditional

A young Parisian designer's dress pattern, to promote DMC sewing thread

styles with his own new ideas his designs have been taken up by some of the biggest buyers in the business, including those at Galeries Lafayette and Bloomingdale's in the States.

The pattern for this exclusive design was offered free at the point of purchase to women buying three reels of Tous Textiles (which they would need to make up the dress) in September, October and November 1989.

This offer was announced on window/in-store posters and, most powerfully of all, on boxes containing 50 free patterns placed on counters.

Results

Seven hundred and forty outlets (from a possible universe of 2000) accepted the promotion and used at least one box of 50 patterns.

Agency: Stag Promotional Campaigns

COMMENT

Tactical objectives for this promotion included selling in a minimum of 200 reels per outlet, accelerating stock turnover, encouraging shop staff to specify DMC etc. In all these respects the promotion was professionally planned and successfully implemented, with nice touches such as flowers from Interflora for female shop managers/owners placing the minimum order.

Strategically, the promotion positioned Tous Textiles as *the* brand for fashion-conscious younger women, interested in clothes that are innovative but 'safe'. The dress patterns represent an excellent example of how inexpensive paper and ink can be given enormous added value by the form they are worked into. These patterns offered DMC's target market immediate entry into the highly aspirational world of successful young designers.

The importance of this brand-enhancing rather than incentive role for the promotion is highlighted by the absence of the word 'FREE!'.

6

LIFESTYLE

INTRODUCTION

Maybe in some less sophisticated time past consumers bought a brand because of its 'USP', its 'unique selling proposition'. Certainly, much advertising in the middle decades of the 20th century sought to identify and communicate some single, functional feature of the brand, some respect in which it could be claimed to outperform competitors. And perhaps in a less prosperous and a more utilitarian era the superior utility of a brand was the right thing to emphasize.

Today's European consumers are spoiled for choice. Brands have to woo them in a more subtle, more friendly, more emotional style. It's no longer enough just to convince them that the brand is apt for its purpose, that it does its job well. They need persuading too that it's right for them, that it will suit them personally, that it's compatible with their tastes in other fields, and that it will fit their lifestyle. A brand has to give evidence that it understands what sort of people it is trying to sell to – not just as consumers of the brand itself, but as rounded human beings with interests, activities, ambitions, anxieties and aspirations over and above those catered for by the brand's functional performance. It's not just a question any longer of a *brand* image: the consumer's *self*-image is equally important in determining whether the sale will be clinched or lost.

Sales promotion can't simply stand aside from these developments. It can't be allowed to go on just simply offering 'unique selling propositions' as to why consumers should buy the promoted brand, at least this month while the offer lasts. Too large a part of marketing support budgets are being devoted to sales promotion to allow it to ignore target consumers' total lifestyles.

Here are some varied examples, then, of brands in different business sectors shaping their promotions to demonstrate that they understand, approve of, and support the wider interests and concerns of their target publics.

THE DICTIONARY THAT GOES CLICK

IL DIZIONARIO CHE SCATTA

BACKGROUND

The Italian publisher, Sansoni Editore, markets a successful range of dictionaries through bookshops/stationers. The best-selling foreign language one is the English dictionary. It faces stiff competition, however, from other publishers' English dictionaries, English being the foreign language most studied by young Italians, both in high schools and in the private English language schools which are big business in the large Italian cities.

Sansoni needed some way of demonstrating to its key target market, teenagers of both sexes, that it was better 'tuned in' to their world than other dictionary publishers.

The English Dictionary that goes 'click' – with a free camera!

THE PROMOTION

A miniature camera was offered free to purchasers of the Sansoni English dictionary.

The camera was packed in a box which simulated the dust-jacket design of the dictionary, and was distributed to bookshops with the dictionary.

The promotion was launched in the autumn of 1990, the period of the year when students are beginning new classes and courses, and lasted through the 1990/1 winter.

The offer was advertised on the Telemontecarlo TV channel, the Radio DJ radio station, in the *Corriere della Sera* newspaper and in the magazines *Espresso* and *In Town*. The headline announced that this was 'The Dictionary that Goes Click!'

Results

The Sansoni English dictionary sold out, supply not quite keeping up with demand.

Agency: Marketing Consultants

COMMENT

Young people are sociable. They go around in groups and 'gangs'. If they are learning English, maybe they will travel abroad together, to London or New York. They are heavily into taking 'snaps' of each other: Gianni and Paola posing on his new motorbike; the whole gang laughing round a café table; Anna and Francesca making funny faces at the Queen's guard in the sentry box near Buckingham Palace, to try to make him smile; Maria holding up her arm and imitating the Statue of Liberty, against a background of the Statue itself. They enjoy having fun together – whereas learning the words of a foreign language from a dictionary is frankly hard work.

With this camera offer, presented in a jokey manner, Sansoni demonstrates its sensitivity towards all these issues.

GET INTO ROCK WITH YOUNG PERSONS' RAIL CARDS

CARTE ET CARRÉ JEUNE VOUS OUVRENT LES VOIES DU ROCK

BACKGROUND

French Railways have two Rail Cards designed for 12–26 year olds. The 'Carte Jeune' offers free travel throughout France during the summer holiday period, June–September. The 'Carré Jeune' allows four rail trips to be made at a discount of 50 per cent, during the course of a year. They cost FFr150 each.

The peak time of the year for selling these cards is May and early June, as summer travel plans are made.

The railways have a particular interest in these younger customers: they represent full-fare paying passengers in the future. It's important to demonstrate to them now that rail travel is convenient, economical and 'OK' – not something you have to keep quiet about to your friends!

THE PROMOTION

French Railways teamed up with the rock group A-HA, in spring 1988, promoting with them at both a national and a regional level.

Regional activities were built round A-HA's concert tour of 15 cities throughout France. Five days before each concert 'hostesses' drove round places where young people gather (restaurants, universities, fast food outlets, cinemas, high schools etc), distributing some 700,000 game cards. These game cards had to be taken to the local railway station and inserted in an electronic machine christened 'Totem', which flashed up on its screen what prizes were won – seats at the forthcoming A-HA concert, tracks of their recent hits or wall posters. Totem machines were sited in 26 railway stations round France, 6 of them in Paris, and alongside each machine was a booth selling the Carte Jeune and the Carré Jeune.

The national promotion ran simultaneously with these regional activities. This national promotion took the form of a mail-in competition, 2,200,000 entry forms being distributed in every French Railways station where 'travellers' tickets' are on sale, from all French Railways

A lifestyle promotion for French Railways' Young Persons Rail Cards

information desks and in some selected travel agencies. Competitors were required to answer questions on both A-HA and these two Young Persons' Rail Cards. Winners toured the 'rock capitals' of the USA for two weeks: New York; Los Angeles; Nashville. Runners up received portable compact-disc players, personal stereos or A-HA cassettes.

To publicize the promotion, clips of A-HA hits, recorded specially for the occasion, were broadcast during the programme *Rock Children* on the A2 channel.

At the end of the promotion, which ran from 1 May until 10 June, French Railways mounted an additional A-HA concert near Paris, offering all 16,000 seats free.

This concert was publicized in the Saint-Lazare and Montparnasse railway stations and by messages on Fun Radio.

Results

Almost one-third of the approximately eight and a half million young French people in the target age group were reached by the entry forms and game cards inviting them to participate in the promotion; 8.28 per cent of the game cards given out by the hostesses in the regions were put through the Totem machines; 2.64 per cent of the national competition entry forms were completed and returned.

Compared with two years earlier, when these two Rail Cards had also been promoted, sales of Carré Jeune increased by 13 per cent and those of Carte Jeune by 20 per cent.

Agency: Marco Polo

COMMENT

Pop music is such an all-pervasive element in youth culture that brands wishing to ingratiate themselves with young people are quick to exploit it, throughout Europe. And it can produce good commercial results.

In Ireland, for example, a 1990 'Twix Rocks' competition offered winners prizes of all-expenses-paid trips to rock concerts of their choice anywhere in Europe, plus runners-up prizes of 30 vouchers for concerts staged in Ireland. Three Twix wrappers were required to enter, and sales increased by 30 per cent during the five-month promotional period. (*Agency: Marketing Network.*)

The Karaoke concept of singing to a pre-recorded backing track was exploited in another Irish promotion in 1990. Bacardi and 7Up was offered as a mixed drink at a special low price in bars frequented by younger customers. Everybody buying this drink had the opportunity to win small prizes such as T-shirts and key-rings (branded to Bacardi or 7Up), and was invited to take the microphone and sing a pop song to a backing track. Over 70 per cent of the clientele purchased a Bacardi and 7Up during these 'Pump up the Volume' evenings. (*Agency: Marketing Network.*)

The French Railways 'Get into Rock' promotion is none the less notable for the extent to which it vigorously exploits the tie-up with the A-HA group. The group was clearly an excellent choice: it's very popular with young people in France and has a 'clean' image which makes it acceptable to their parents – parents still providing the finance for travel for at least the younger teenagers in the target market. And perhaps French Railways could therefore have been forgiven for simply 'sponsoring' the group on its tour of the country, and leaving this association to communicate the compatibility of rail travel with young people's lifestyle. Instead, the tie-up was made to work at every level, with young people being invited to participate actively (importantly by calling in at their local railway station), rather than just sitting back and listening.

POSTSCRIPT

The Carte and Carré Jeune are now renamed 'Carrissimo'.

OTHER YOUTH LIFESTYLE THEMES

The cinema is another aspect of youth culture exploited in a 7Up promotion in France: '1988: 7Up Invents the FFr7 Cinema Ticket' (*'1988: 7Up invente la place de cinéma à 7F'*). Three proofs of purchase and FFr7 worth of stamps were all that were required for a voucher that would admit youngsters to the film of their choice. (*Agency: Cato Johnson.*)

Similarly, in Italy in 1988, M&Ms's TV campaign showing young friends enjoying the product in the cinema was backed by a promotion '*M&Ms Vi Porta al Cinema*' ('M&Ms take you to the cinema'). Four proofs of purchase qualified for entry to a lottery to win four tickets to take friends along to the cinema. (*Agency: The Sales Machine Italia.*)

Sports and outdoor activities – sometimes of a distinctly machismo character – are another popular theme with promoters of products and services that have young men as a prime audience. In Britain Gillette Right Guard Sport invited them to 'Try a New Sport' in a 1987 promotion. Simply by showing a pack of Gillette Right Guard Sport at major regional sports centres throughout the country, the purchaser was entitled to enjoy a whole range of sporting activities entirely free. (*Agency: Option One.*)

In Spain Ford marked the launch of the XR2i in 1990 by inviting men aged 18–35 years to fill up entry forms with their personal driving/ motoring details, to participate in a sweepstake in which 250 winners received high-speed driving tuition on the Jarama race track, the 15 showing the most aptitude being invited to participate in the 'XR2i Formula Grandprix'. (*Agency: Promotional Campaigns.*)

In Holland the 'Marlboro Challenge '88' similarly offered the chance to motor race, tying in with the brand's sponsorship of Formula 1. Candidates passing a paper test were then tested on their driving skills. The three best were offered a racing course and the very best a one-year sponsorship by Marlboro of approximately DFl100,000 (*Agency: Bridge/ KLP.*)

In France, again in 1988, Drakkar Noir invited young men to '*Défiez Vos Limites*' ('Push Yourself Beyond the Limit') by organizing for them practice with Formula 3000 cars, off-shore power boats, speed sailing or skiing down the piste used to establish a world speed record. (*Agency: GMS.*)

THE TEAM ENGRAVED ON YOUR HEART

LA SQUADRA DEL CUORE

BACKGROUND

Be warned, women from Northern Europe! That romantic attention you get from Italian men means very little: their real passion is football, *and sooner or later they're going to desert you in favour of watching or talking about the game. X-ray the average Italian male's heart and what do you find engraved on it: the name of a wife or mistress? Don't you believe it: it'll be his favourite football team!*

This centrality of football in the leisure lives of Italian men was put to brilliant use in a 1987 promotion for IP (Italiana Petroli) petrol stations.

'*Vote for the Team Engraved on Your Heart*'

THE PROMOTION

Motorists pulling into any one of IP's petrol stations, throughout Italy, were invited to vote for their favourite football team. All teams were eligible, from the world-famous clubs of the Italian first division down to the local village team. A voting slip was handed to every motorist who visited an IP petrol station. The whole petrol forecourt was dressed out as a voting station, with an 'urn' in which the motorist could record his vote instantly. The 'election' took place over a three-month period.

Here was a chance for every supporter to 'play' for his team, rather than just watching the team play for him, since considerable prestige would attach to the team receiving the most votes and being awarded the *'Squadra del Cuore'* trophy at the end of the campaign.

And there was something in it for the fan too: randomly-drawn voting slips won weekly prizes such as trips to that season's European Cup final in Vienna and vouchers for 1000 litres of IP petrol; plus final prizes of the means to buy a house, a motorboat and – since some women would be voting too – a magnificent fur coat.

Quite apart from the impact of IP petrol forecourts – all 6000 of them – carrying these exhortations to 'Vote!' the campaign also received heavy support in other media, notably television. For example, Maria Teresa Ruta, the elegant and athletic journalist pictured on all the forecourt displays, had a TV slot every Sunday evening in *La Domenica Sportiva* ('Sport on Sunday'), in which she presented a team from the Italian league, showed high spots in their recent history and got illustrious fans talking about their passion for the team.

Results

Enormous interest was generated by this intriguing election campaign. It became a big talking point in bars and cafés round the country, and received much journalistic comment in the media.

More than 65 million votes were cast – a truly astonishing figure in a country of only 56 million people (men, women and children). This was Italy's biggest-ever referendum, by a very wide margin!

Juventus received most votes (13,505,331), Napoli the second highest number (9,961,229). Election results were published with both national totals and regional breakdowns, and were no doubt pored over and argued over by the fans of both the popular and the less popular teams.

The promotion positioned IP firmly in the forefront of support for Italy's favourite game, tying in with and supporting IP's exclusive sponsorship of its own *'Squadra del Cuore'*, the Italian national team, then busy qualifying for the 1990 World Cup finals, to be played (where else?) in Italy.

Agency: Promarco Advertising

COMMENT

So is this really a sales promotion or rather a PR campaign of enormous proportions? Does it matter? Remember the *Superman* films: 'Is it a bird? Is it a plane? It's Superman!'.

'La Squadra del Cuore' qualifies as Superpromotion!

No one company, no single brand, can ever quite own sole property rights on as big an interest area as football, but this promotion shows IP coming as close to doing so as anyone has to date. Even sub-audiences, secondary to adult males, were wooed. We've mentioned the fur coat prize already and some well-known women were interviewed on *La Domenica Sportiva*, revealing that they too were fans of a particular team. Similarly a slot for *La Squadra del Cuore* was taken in another popular TV entertainment programme, *'Drive In'*, on Sunday evenings, to reach a wider public than the more fanatical sports enthusiasts.

Other brands will none the less stake out smaller claims to football in its differing roles for specific target markets.

FOOTBALL AND OTHER TARGET AUDIENCES

It's not just *adult* men who are passionate about football: boys are too, from as young as maybe five or six years of age. And unlike most of their fathers, they *play* the game as well as watch it.

Ringo biscuits have a role as a snack between meals for Italian boys when they're meeting up with their friends, other 'Ringo Boys', especially to play sports. 'The Great Ringo Five-a-Side Cup' (*'La Grande Partita di Ringo'*) was a two-day tournament held in July 1990 at one of the Italian World Cup team's retreats. Boys qualified to compete by sending in just two proofs of purchase from Ringo. When an entry was 'drawn out of the hat', the boy sending it was invited to bring along four of his friends to form one of 24 five-a-side teams, divided into groups according to ages (6 to 17 years). All boys competing were able to keep the football kit and footballs provided by Ringo. (*Agency: Inventa.*)

Nor is it just the men in the family who are affected by a big footballing event like the 1990 World Cup final. In the UK Safeway grocery stores showed their sensitivity to the disruptive impact on wives' and mothers' lives by offering them a 'World Cup Survivor's Guide'! Containing advice on how to cope with males 'glued' to their TV sets while the matches were being broadcast and able to talk of nothing else except football in between, the 'Guide' offered quick and easy recipes for meals snatched during the breaks, jobs for husbands and sons to do between matches, a pull-out match schedule and coupons redeemable against the types of food and drink most suitable for consumption during this fraught period. There was even a competition for women to win a trip to Italy – *not* to watch the World Cup matches, however, but to enjoy a more restful and romantic stay in Verona and Merano. (*Agency: Promotional Campaigns.*)

MAKE THE MOST OF FAMILY DAY

FAMILIENTAG — ERLEBNISTAG

BACKGROUND

In 1988 the woman who was then Minister for Families in the German government decreed that the third Sunday in every October should be 'Family Day'. It was to be a day when all generations of a family should get together to celebrate in each other's company. It proved a popular idea: a 1990 survey showed 85 per cent of Germans to be in favour of the idea.

With the family clearly occupying such an important role in everybody's thoughts (at least for this one day a year!), it was clearly a powerful lifestyle theme (and occasion) for products and services to associate themselves with.

'Family Day' in Germany

THE PROMOTION

Family Day fell on 20 October in 1991. A month earlier a 16-page magazine entitled *Make the Most of Family Day (Familientag – Erlebnistag)* was inserted in three and a half million copies of *Funk-Uhr* (a weekly radio and TV programme guide).

A series of double-page spreads reported on how various celebrities planned to spend Family Day, gave recipes for meals ranging from buffet brunch to a formal sit-down dinner, explained how to make various cocktails and described a number of games for the family to play together.

Participating brands were mentioned where appropriate in the recipes, eg Kellogg's Corn Flakes, Hohes C Vitamin Drink, Jacobs Krönung Coffee, Söhnlein Brillant Aperitif, Eckes Edelkirsch, Milka Chocolat etc.

These 'advertorial' features provided the context for a series of promotional offers requiring only telephone calls from the reader to win flowers (as gifts or table decorations), brunch baskets, seats at the circus, restaurant meals, party ideas books and video cameras – all designed to enhance the pleasure of Family Day.

Jacobs Krönung Coffee, the main sponsor of this promotion, offered as prizes in one of these telephone draws expenses-paid family trips to a big Family Day show in the Europa theme park at Rust in Baden. There, one of the families was to be 'drawn out of a hat' and named 'Krönung Family of the Year', and sent off on a free trip round the world.

Results

Approximately 100,000 telephone calls were received, entering for the various prizes.

Market share of the main sponsor, Jacobs Krönung Coffee, increased by 15 per cent during the promotion period, compared with the previous year's average.

Agency: Focus Interaktion

COMMENT

Playing a leading role in *the* day of the year for families clearly helped position these brands as 'right for the family' for other days too, above all for the mother in her everyday role as purchaser/provider for the family.

LET'S PLANT A WHOLE FOREST FOR ITALY

PIANTIAMO UNA FORESTA PER L'ITALIA

BACKGROUND

Threats to the environment have become big political and commercial issues throughout Western Europe. Electorates demonstrate their support for political action by casting votes for 'Green' candidates, and other political parties feel impelled to show sensitivity to the issues. Consumers try to avoid ecologically harmful products and buy those which do not pollute the environment. Behaving in environmentally friendly ways has become an important part of the lifestyle of many contemporary Europeans.

Here is just one example of a sales promotion which demonstrates sympathy and active support for such behaviour. It is concerned with anxieties about global deforestation (the destruction of the rain forests, for example) and its possible implications for global warming.

Lysoform, a Lever product, is a very long-established brand leader in the liquid household cleaner/disinfectant sector in Italy. It is used on floors and other surfaces, and it comes in two alternative varieties: 'regular' or with deodorizing pine perfume. As the brand has always been classified as a medical/surgical product by the Italian authorities, Lysoform has not been allowed to offer the consumer inducements to purchase.

The authorities relaxed their usual restrictions for the following 1990 promotion, which was seen as being clearly for the public good.

THE PROMOTION

Lysoform funded the planting of 50,000 trees in four regions of Italy. The areas were selected as being in special need of reforestation by Italia Nostra ('Our Italy'), an organization dedicated to the preservation of Italy's heritage, both man-made and natural. Italia Nostra took responsibility for supervising the planting and ensuring the young trees were protected during the first year. As the advertising for this initiative said,

Sì, piantiamola!
Per riassestare il verde, per aiutare l'ecosistema, per migliorare l'ambiente.
Lysoform, per cominciare, offre 50.000 piante: non è la soluzione definitiva dei problemi dell'ambiente in Italia, ma è un passo avanti, un passo al quale tutti possono partecipare, anche tu.
Come? Taglia, compila e spedisci in busta chiusa questo coupon, o la cartolina che trovi nei migliori supermercati a: Lysoform Operazione Ambiente - c/o Lever - c.p. 10502 - 20100 Milano; incollando nell'apposito spazio il sigillo di garanzia presente sui flaconi di Lysoform detergente liquido per pavimenti; per ogni cartolina/coupon pervenuti entro il 15 settembre 1990, pianteremo un albero in più (fino ad un massimo di altri 50.000 alberi).
Dove? In una delle zone segnalate da Italia Nostra, l'Associazione Nazionale per la tutela del patrimonio storico, artistica e naturale italiana: l'isola d'Elba, le sponde del Po, le Alpi del bellunese e l'entroterra amalfitano, zone in cui Italia Nostra si impegna a curarli ancora per un anno dopo la messa a dimora.
Allora, vogliamo fare qualcosa per l'Italia, tutti insieme?

Cognome _____
Nome _____
Via _____ n. _____
Città _____
Provincia _____ CAP _____
Telefono _____

Sì, voglio partecipare anch'io a questa grande iniziativa "Lysoform-Operazione Ambiente", in collaborazione con **Italia Nostra**, l'Associazione Nazionale per la tutela del patrimonio storico, artistico e naturale italiano. Vi invio quindi questo coupon, debitamente compilato, sapendo che per ogni coupon pervenuto verrà piantato un albero (fino ad un massimo di 50.000 in aggiunta agli altri 50.000 alberi offerti da Lysoform) in una delle zone segnalate da **Italia Nostra**: Isola d'Elba, sponde del Po, Alpi del bellunese ed entroterra amalfitano.

Applicare qui il sigillo di garanzia

Piantiamo una foresta per l'Italia.

In Collaborazione con Italia Nostra

Lysoform Casa, Lysoform Casa Deodorante profumo di Pino, disinfettanti e detergenti liquidi per pavimenti e altre superfici.

'Let's Plant a Forest for Italy'

'It's by no means a complete solution to Italy's environmental problems but it's a step in the right direction'.

The public were invited to join in and help: 'Let's Plant a Whole Forest for Italy' read headlines in press advertisements. The advertisements carried application forms (or application cards were inserted in the same publications), and Lysoform guaranteed to plant an *additional* tree for every application sent in, completed and validated with a proof of purchase of Lysoform.

Further application cards were made available at the point of purchase.

Results

Consumers sent numerous letters expressing goodwill for the promotion and the brand.

Approximately 50,000 application forms/cards were received, each resulting in the planting of an extra tree. This was seen as quite a high level considering that the individual consumer received no direct, personal benefit, and in view of the fact that production constraints had prevented the promotion being announced on Lysoform bottles.

Agency: The Sales Machine Italia

COMMENT

The whole of Lysoform's advertising in the first half of 1990 was devoted to announcing and describing this initiative: for a brand much constrained by its classification as a medical product, this promotion represented a topical, newsworthy talking point.

Similarly, the permission to promote, which this environmental project obtained, provided an opportunity to gain greater stand-out than usual for the brand at the point of purchase.

7

BUDGET STRETCHING

INTRODUCTION

Co-promotions, in which a brand or company combines resources with one or more partners, can help a promotional budget stretch further and work harder.

An example is the 'Make the Most of Family Day' promotion we looked at in Chapter 6, where the participating brands were able to mount a much larger and more ambitious promotion together than their individual budgets would have financed alone. Similarly, Johnson Wax would not have been able to afford to demonstrate its One Step shoe polish to so many prospects, had it not joined forces with the Boy Scouts Association, as we saw in Chapter 3.

Here are some more examples, from across Europe, where a careful choice of promotional partners shares costs, swops resources and gives access to the partner's consumers.

FREE CHALET WINE WHEN YOU PAY WITH DINERS' CARD

BACKGROUND

A leading wine bottler, Kourtakis, launched Chalet white wine in Greece, in early 1990. Chalet was designed to offer high quality at a price affordable to those medium- and high-income consumers at whom it was aimed.

Tasks, at launch, included getting Chalet into distribution, especially in large chains, announcing this new wine to these target consumers and inducing them to try it.

Alpha-Beta is one of the largest and most progressive modern supermarket chains in Greece, carrying a wide variety of high-quality products. It was of prime importance that it should stock Chalet.

'Pay with Diners and we give you a bottle of Chalet' says this mailing to card holders in Greece, launching this new wine in Alpha-Beta supermarkets

THE PROMOTION

Shoppers spending at least Dr12,000 in any of the 15 Alpha-Beta stores and paying by Diners' Card were handed a free bottle of Chalet wine.

Alpha-Beta checkouts were supplied with special Chalet Wine Diners vouchers. The shopper's card was run through the machine once to validate the standard voucher for the purchases and then a second time to validate the Free Chalet Wine voucher, a copy of this going back to Kourtakis to confirm that the free bottle had been correctly used.

The offer lasted for 20 days and was announced by direct mail to Diners' Club members in Greece, and by displays in Alpha-Beta stores.

Results

Approximately 5000 bottles of Chalet were given away to qualifying shoppers in the 15 stores during the 20-day promotional period.

Agency: Win Communications

COMMENT

Diners' Club members were the perfect target market for Chalet wine.

Chalet wine was a very appropriate premium for Diners' Club to offer its members to encourage them to use their Diners' Card when shopping at Alpha-Beta stores – rather than paying cash or using a competitor's charge or credit card.

Alpha-Beta stores were willing to stock and display this new brand of wine, confident that this promotion to Diners' Club members would produce a demand for it, and happy to have a free bottle of wine to offer as a gift to their shoppers, financed by Kourtakis.

This was an excellent example of the mutuality of interest of three different parties being served by a single, simple offer.

GIVE YOUR CHILD THE BEST START WITH COLGATE

COLGATE GIV DIT BARN DKR25 PÅ EN JUNIORKONTO

BACKGROUND

With its two main brands, Colgate Regular and Colgate Blue Minty Gel, accounting for more than half of all sales of toothpaste in Denmark in 1989, the Colgate company might have been forgiven for sitting back and 'resting on its laurels'.

However, for this success to continue Colgate needed to make constant efforts to build brand loyalty among families with children under 15. Such families, with their above-average number of family members, were already important purchasers of toothpaste: the parents were by definition still young, with many years of teeth cleaning ahead of them, and most important of all the children represented tomorrow's consumers, stretching far into the future. Habits formed in childhood can sometimes last a lifetime.

Cleaning teeth is a serious business. Some children may find it a bore, but their mothers will keep them at it knowing that their dental health in later life is dependent to a large extent on proper care for their teeth when young. What's more it's the mothers who buy toothpaste for the family.

It was mothers, therefore, to whom Colgate needed to make their prime appeal, emphasizing the benefit they delivered in terms of setting children up for the future, giving them 'the best start' in life.

THE PROMOTION

Children under 15, with their mothers' help, were invited to open a junior savings account with Privatbanken, Denmark's third-largest bank. Privatbanken offered a deposit of DKr25 to start the account in return for five tokens from special promotional packs of Colgate toothpastes.

These promotional tokens were printed on Colgate and Colgate Blue Minty Gel, shrink-wrapped as twin-packs. Three twin-packs were therefore required to obtain the five tokens to qualify for the DKr25 deposit, leaving the mother with a spare token to encourage her, perhaps, to start collecting for a second deposit for a second child.

Køb
Colgate
og giv dit
barn kr. 25,-
på en
Juniorkonto

The promotion was announced by displays in outlets stocking Colgate toothpastes, and displays in every branch of Privatbanken. Advertisements or inserts in four weekly magazines read by mothers and in the *Donald Duck* children's magazine reached 70 per cent of Danish households.

A month into the promotion full-page advertisements in Danish newspapers, reaching 65 per cent of all parents, acted as reminders to keep on saving their tokens.

Five tokens from Colgate toothpastes opened a savings account for a child with a leading Danish bank

Results

Sales of Colgate toothpastes were up 25 per cent within three months of the promotion starting.

Over 10,000 junior accounts were opened in these three months by Privatbanken, a 100 per cent increase on the usual rate.

Agency: Cato Johnson

COMMENT

The offer was reasonably generous in monetary terms in the sense that DKr25 represented approximately half the cost of buying three twin-packs. At minimum, therefore, it was good for Colgate to have this equivalent of a cash refund financed by their partner, Privatbanken.

Much more important was the form this cash took: it was for the child, rather than the parent and, in particular, it was for the child's future. We can reasonably hypothesize therefore that the families that participated were families of key interest and potential for both Colgate and Privatbanken: families bringing up their children to act responsibly in terms of the future, rather than seeking only present gratification.

Win a Fortune with your Number Plate

Un Tesoro Targato Italia

Background

Italy has a flourishing magazine industry, with a wide range of titles catering for a wide variety of interests and tastes. The constant launching of new titles means that well-established, general interest magazines have to work hard to maintain, let alone improve, their position.

Famiglia Cristiana *('Christian Family') is a notably well-established magazine. Published weekly by San Paolo Periodici, it commanded a circulation of over a million copies in early 1990. Almost half of these were sold through churches, one-third through subscriptions and only roughly one-fifth through newsstands, the main 'battleground' for most magazines.*

Readership was high, at about six million, covering members of the family in the 30–75 age group.

It was decided to make a determined drive to add a younger, more modern, more dynamic readership, which in practice meant increasing sales above all through newsstands.

The Promotion

Every week, from January through April 1990, *Famiglia Cristiana* published a five-figure number. The reader was invited to compare this number with the first five figures of the registration number of the reader's car. If they matched the reader won a share of L30 million worth of Agip petrol coupons, divided equally among all winners each week. There was a second chance to win, for those whose car registration numbers did not match: readers completing and mailing in an entry form in the magazine were entered in a lottery with a weekly prize of a Renault 19 Chamade.

In parallel with this promotion, from February to April, motorists stopping at any one of Agip's approximately 7500 petrol stations were given a sealed envelope, containing a five-figure number. If this number matched that published that week in *Famiglia Cristiana*, the motorist won Agip petrol coupons to a value of L500,000. And again there was a second chance to win a Renault 19 Chamade in a lottery.

Car number plates were 'lucky numbers' in this Italian joint promotion

To reach an even wider audience with news of these linked promotions, Enrica Bonaccorti, the presenter of the Canale 5 TV programme, *Cari Genitori* ('Dear Parents') chatted about it to her viewers every day.

Results

Sales through newsstands increased by 40 per cent.

Agency: Promotions Italia

COMMENT

Agip's interest in building traffic and the magazine's interest in building circulation were most efficiently combined in this promotion, each partner making available to the other its very large clientele.

Notice how 'lucky numbers' were made much more interesting and less anonymous by relating them to the reader's own individual car registration number.

8

DISTRIBUTION AND DISPLAY

INTRODUCTION

Our case studies have so far concentrated on promoting to the *consumer*. For good reason: in affluent European societies, where abundance and even oversupply are commonplace, it's the consumer who wields power and influence.

However, the consumer can buy goods and services only when they are made readily available through retail outlets. And as such retail outlets are usually under the separate ownership of distribution specialists, suppliers commonly put sales promotion to work to help achieve *trade* objectives too, at minimum to ensure their products are stocked in distributors' outlets; better still, to persuade distributors to present or in some way display these products so as to draw special attention to them.

Giving a consumer promotion an additional trade 'angle' can be an especially effective way of achieving these trade objectives. The distributor is reassured that time and money spent on the brand and space devoted to it will be justified by the extra sales the consumer offer will stimulate.

One such trade 'angle' was that adopted by Heinz at the time of the 'Heinz 100 Day Driveaway' in 1990 (see page 85). This was to 'tailor' this big budget, nationwide promotion to retail chains' individual requirements, as part of negotiations designed to secure off-shelf display.

Typically, further Metro cars were offered as prizes in competitions exclusive to shoppers in an individual multiple chain. For example:

- chain 'A' shoppers were invited to use their skill and judgement to rank eight attributes of the Metro in order of importance;
- chain 'B' shoppers were invited to solve a motoring word-finder puzzle;

- chain 'C' shoppers were invited to rank in order of importance eight items to take on a family holiday in the Metro;
- chain 'D' shoppers were invited to spot the differences on twó maps;
- chain 'E' shoppers were invited to answer multiple-choice questions about the length of six British motorways.

Second prizes in these various tailored competitions included Heinz/AA Road Atlases, Heinz First Aid Kits and Heinz Car Care Kits. And usually there were further prizes of grocery vouchers, redeemable, of course, only in the chain running the competition.

Here are some more hardworking – sometimes spectacular – case studies of achieving trade objectives through consumer promotions.

CARLSBERG LEISURE GUIDES
GUÍA CARLSBERG DEL TIEMPO LIBRE

BACKGROUND

The best-selling brand of imported beer in Spanish bars and restaurants in 1990 was Heineken. Carlsberg was second. Its distribution in particularly middlemarket and upmarket bars was good, but it needed to draw greater attention to itself, to obtain some form of display, to achieve a strong, continuing and active 'presence' in these bars.

THE PROMOTION

Carlsberg published a series of 'Leisure Guides', one for each major Spanish city, detailing 'what's on and where', and telling you all you needed to know about local exhibitions, theatres, concerts, cinema programmes, fairs, shows and other leisure entertainments.

These Leisure Guides were free, and typically 30–40 were placed in special display holders on bars and on tables by the Carlsberg sales force.

Each issue of the Guide gave information about a single month's activities, and initially three issues were made in May, June and July 1990.

Results

In an important sense this promotion would succeed only if bar owners permitted the first issue of the Guides to be placed on their premises, observed their clientele to be taking an interest in them, and therefore requested further issues.

They did! To such an extent that publication of the guides was extended for a further year, September 1990 to August 1991.

Agency: Promocion y Comunicacion

COMMENT

The Guides were described on their front pages as being presented by Carlsberg *and* the bar in which it was being read, making both a more integral part of the leisure scene.

Guía **Carlsberg**

EDICION GRATUITA

1-31 Julio   Del tiempo libre

M A L A G A

En el año 1847 el maestro cervecero J.C. Jacobsen inició en Dinamarca la elaboración de la cerveza CARLSBERG, nombre dado en honor de su hijo Carl.

J.C. Jacobsen se adelantó a su tiempo consagrando toda una filosofía: calidad y perfección. Esta filosofía convirtió a CARLSBERG en la primera fábrica de cerveza del mundo que empezó utilizando la levadura pura en la fabricación de la cerveza.

El nombre de CARLSBERG, a través de toda su historia, es sinónimo de cerveza de calidad y prestigio. Su presencia en más de 150 países del mundo, constata su internacionalidad.

CARLSBERG como primera marca de cerveza internacional, presente en los acontecimientos mundiales más importantes, quiere dar a conocer a sus consumidores las actividades más destacadas que ocurren en su ciudad. Por ello CARLSBERG y este establecimiento han realizado la Guía CARLSBERG del tiempo libre, para informarle mientras saborea una CARLSBERG, de lo que hay que saber sobre su ciudad para estar al día.

Carlsberg Leisure Guides were distributed in Spanish bars and restaurants

FUTURISTIC ELECTRONICS WITH OGGI IN TAVOLA

L'ELETTRONICA FUTURISTA DI OGGI IN TAVOLA

BACKGROUND

Oggi in Tavola ('Today's Menu') is a range of pre-cooked convenience foods, especially first courses or 'starters'. The quality of the ingredients is excellent, the taste is 'contemporary', and the packaging is bright, modern and youthful.

Oggi in Tavola is marketed in Italy by Italgel for those who are short of time but need to put together something special quickly, or who simply want to enjoy a straightforward but well-prepared classic Italian dish.

The target market is therefore working housewives from 25 onwards, young people living on their own and young couples.

In early 1991 the range was still new and little known. The requirement was to draw very strong attention to Oggi in Tavola at the point of purchase, to encourage first-time trial. As special displays are just as difficult to negotiate in Italian foodstores as elsewhere in Europe, something extra special was required. And, to communicate the brand's modernity, it needed to be something innovative.

THE PROMOTION

Sited by the brand in-store was an electronic gaming machine, periodically flashing lights and emitting space-age sounds.

Shoppers could win prizes of various values by playing this machine. To do so they were required to purchase Oggi in Tavola, after which they were handed a sealed card by a promotion girl. Opening this revealed a number, and tapping this number into the machine activated it.

There was a second chance to win prizes (this time of small household electrical appliances) by mailing in this same card, with two proofs of purchase of Oggi in Tavola, to participate in a lottery.

This sealed card contained a unique number which activated an electronic gaming machine in Italian hypermarkets

Results

The electronic gaming machines were sited in over 20 hypermarkets between March and May 1991.

They attracted great attention and 48 per cent of shoppers who asked how the machines worked bought Oggi in Tavola in order to play them.

Sales of Oggi in Tavola increased by anything between 20 per cent and 300 per cent, this variation depending above all on the location of the store and the character of its shoppers.

Agency: Inventa

COMMENT

An invitation to get involved with a piece of contemporary technology can gain exceptional levels of acceptance from the trade, and exceptional levels of attention from the consumer, especially when it's as entertaining and user-friendly as this was.

MASTERPIECES BY JAVEL LA CROIX

JAVEL LA CROIX: C'EST TOUT UN ART

BACKGROUND

Colgate Palmolive's Javel La Croix commanded a dominant share of some 76 per cent of the French bleach market in early 1990. However, the brand was under pressure from competitors such as Saint-Marc, Bref and various own-label bleaches.

What was needed was a memorable campaign which would reinforce the brand's position as market leader, communicate its versatility in performing a number of different disinfecting jobs around the house and do so in a way which enhanced Javel La Croix's reputation for quality, without taking itself too seriously.

Eight famous paintings were subtly adapted to show various uses for Javel La Croix bleach

THE PROMOTION

Eight famous paintings were selected, each featuring women and illustrating a different application for Javel La Croix: disinfecting;

bleaching; stain removal; deodorizing etc. The paintings were:

- *The Washerwoman* by Chardin;
- *Madame Recamier* by David;
- *The Ironers* by Degas;
- *The Washerwomen* by Fragonard;
- *The Siesta* by Gauguin;
- *Jeanne Avril Dancing* by Toulouse Lautrec;
- *Sunflowers* by Van Gogh;
- *The Letter* by Vermeer.

Two of France's top commercial artists, Darigo and Lermite, were specially commissioned to produce a series of copies, skilfully weaving Javel La Croix into the fabric of the originals. New titles, making housewives the heroines of the paintings were added: Mrs Degas cleans her linen, Mrs Gauguin washes her floors and so on.

Week-long exhibitions of the paintings were staged in six leading hypermarkets across France. Each exhibition was presented on a purpose-built 60 m² stand. Hostesses gave each visitor a commemorative poster of the exhibition, and a booklet on the different uses and applications of Javel La Croix. Before each show opened posters announcing the exhibition were displayed in upmarket boutiques and clothes shops in the surrounding area, ensuring stylish pre-publicity. And as a preview for the whole campaign a press show was staged in Paris at the Chatelet Victoria.

Agency: Cato Johnson

COMMENT

This was very much a brand leader promotion: confident, bold and ambitious.

It's all about reasserting Javel La Croix's dominance, not least at the point of purchase. Not many promotions justify an in-store exhibition!

ESCAPE FROM SHARK ISLAND

BACKGROUND

The LEGO range's position as Britain's best-selling toy has in part been achieved by an on-going programme of imaginative product development and innovation. In 1989 LEGO Pirates were launched, to add new interest and play possibilities to a range already including themes such as Town, Space, Castle, Train, Ship etc.

LEGO Pirates were chosen to spearhead the summer 1990 campaign. A sales target was set, similar to what was sold-in at the launch of Pirates a year earlier – not easy to achieve since typically sales have turned down in the second year.

The key to success was going to be to create maximum activity at the point of purchase, where retailers could see it for themselves, giving them the confidence to place orders and indeed assisting sell-through.

Such in-store activity needed to take account of the widely different sizes of outlets stocking LEGO toys.

THE PROMOTION

Children aged 5-13 were invited to 'Escape from Shark Island'. Here's the copy on an in-store leaflet, setting the scene:

Imagine you are Jimbo, the Cabin Boy from the LEGO Pirates Television Commercial, and you have been washed overboard in high seas, just as you were about to encounter Governor Broadside's Galleon, *The Sea Hawk.*

You find yourself alone, a castaway on the shores of a desert island, but you do not know who or what may be lurking in the jungle close by!

The *Dark Shark Ship* can just be seen sailing away on the horizon, immediately your thoughts turn to escape, but how? You start searching frantically for bits and pieces washed up on the shore ... but cannot find anything. Suddenly you trip over something buried in the sand ... it looks like an old treasure chest! You dig it up and open it ... inside there are hundreds of LEGO bricks!

Your heart races with excitement and suddenly you realize that this treasure chest was left by one of the last poor inhabitants of the island, who had planned to build an escape craft. But did they make it? Perhaps the sharks got them ... just one of the many dangers when you ...

Escape from Shark Island!

*This 'Escape from Shark Island' promotion created maximum in-store activity for
LEGO Pirates*

The precise form taken by this invitation to 'escape' differed according to the size and number of staff available in the store.

In some 80 department stores or large specialist toy retailers, LEGO bricks were provided for children to build an 'Escape Craft' of their own imagining and design in the store.

Approximately 250 independent toy retailers invited children to build their escape craft at home, using their own bricks, and then bring it into the store.

All children who built a model received a 'Captain Roger's Building Diploma'.

In addition, other leaflets were made available in some 2000 further outlets where limited space and/or staffing levels made such in-store building or receiving of models impossible. Here, children had the chance to judge on which of three alternative rafts Jimbo escaped, and to name his escape craft.

Escape craft built by children were used to enhance in-store and window displays. And in all cases there were prizes to be won: LEGO Pirates sets in each store for the best and most imaginative models, built in-store or at home (categorized into two age groups, 5–8 and 9–12), plus a family trip to the LEGOLAND Theme Park in Denmark for a national winner in each category, judged on photographs submitted by the stores. And there was a family trip to LEGOLAND too for the winner of the third competition, to identify and name Jimbo's escape craft on the leaflet.

Throughout the summer period of this promotion, LEGO Pirates were advertised on television. A strong package of point of purchase materials featured Jimbo the Pirate Boy. Retailers were encouraged to advertise their building competitions in the local press and LEGO UK provided artwork for this purpose.

Results

All LEGO Pirates retailers participated in the promotion, in one of its three alternative forms, described above.

The sell-in of LEGO Pirates much exceeded target and was 39 per cent higher than was achieved one year earlier, at launch.

Agency: (In-house)

COMMENT

This was a highly motivating promotion for children: not only was it fun building an escape craft, it was great to have it put on display, perhaps even in the shop window, with one's own name on the tag for all to see.

And because it was going to prove so popular with their young customers, it was reasonable to ask retailers to devote this exceptional amount of space, time and effort to this promotion.

GRANDMOTHERS' DAY

LA FÊTE DES GRAND'MÈRES

BACKGROUND

'Grandmothers' Day' was introduced in France in March 1986, at the initiative of the company marketing the Grand'mère range of coffees. Since then Grandmothers' Day has been the subject of a vigorous public relations and paid-for advertising campaign. This has included, to highlight just a few typical activities from recent years:

- *franking of mail in main post offices with a reminder of the date of Grandmothers' Day;*

- *school essay competitions – 'My Grandmother is Fantastic';*

- *'sponsoring' of big audience television programmes about Grandmothers' Day on the TF1 channel, with well-known presenters such as Patrick Sabatier and Jean-Pierre Foucault;*

- *tie-ins with florists – for example, every bouquet bought for grandmother results in a FFr2 donation to a children's charity;*

- *tie-ins with pâtisseries – for example 'Win a delicious cake in this store'.*

Today Grandmothers' Day is firmly established in the calendar, with a 1991 survey indicating that over three-quarters of the French population know about it, and that more than one French grand-mother in every two is involved in some form of celebration on this, their own, special day.

The role of sales promotion has been to transfer the success of these public relations activities to the point of purchase of Cafés Grand'mère. They are not claiming credit for Grandmothers' Day, but on the contrary exploiting the event as if it existed independently of the brand – which indeed it now does.

Grandmothers' Day, at the point of purchase

THE PROMOTIONS

Various promotional themes have been used at the point of purchase. For example:

- 1992 – 'Tell your Grandmother you Love Her' (the offer of free phone calls);
- 1991 – 'Make a Wish – Cafés Grand'mère will grant it on Grandmothers' Day';

- 1990 – 'Celebrate Grandmothers' Day with Champagne and Chocolates';
- 1989 – 'Share with Grandmother the Three Secrets of a Really Successful Celebration';
- 1988 – 'Make your Grandmother's Most Cherished Dream Come True'.

These promotional concepts have been shaped and adapted to different sizes of grocery store in what is now a 'classic' pattern:

- hypermarkets – winners in each store resulting from some special in-store activity/event;
- supermarkets – winners in each store and shoppers participate in a nationwide competition;
- superettes – winners for shoppers in each multiple chain or voluntary group.

The 1990 display illustrated is a typical example of what has been achieved in hypermarkets. Cafés Grand'mère promotion girls handed out game cards to shoppers entering the store, directing them to the coffee gondola end. Here the card was inserted in an electronic gaming machine: if it was a winner the promotion girl awarded the prize, champagne or chocolates for grandmother, on the spot.

Considerable creativity has been invested in communicating these promotional activities to the grocery trade in a forceful and memorable manner. In 1989, for example, details of the planned activities were 'printed' on 'pages' made of unleavened bread and marzipan – the world's first-ever edible sales presenter!

Results

In recent years off-shelf displays for Cafés Grand'mère have been achieved in some 90 per cent of grocery stores targeted for such displays. In 1991, for example, gondola end displays were mounted in more than 5000 outlets, in the ten days or so leading up to Grandmothers' Day – an exceptional number which translated immediately into record market shares for the various coffees in the Cafés Grand'mère range.

Agency: CL,A (now ECCLA)

COMMENT

Gaining a regular annual prime 'slot' in the distributive trade's promotional programme is worth a great deal to any fmcg brand. In many sectors extra display equals extra sales.

Cafés Grand'mère's route to achieving this – creating a new 'red-letter day' in the calendar – was extremely ambitious but outstandingly successful.

9

PAN-EUROPEAN
PROMOTIONS

INTRODUCTION

THE EUROPEAN BRAND

Many multinational corporations market the same brand or brands in a number of different European countries. Sometimes a single, identical brand name is employed. Sometimes the name differs from country to country, but the brand proposition is identical across Europe. And sometimes, to illustrate the undoubted complexity of this question of European brands, the same brand name is used for a product, but in practice its role and positioning versus competitors differs in different countries. It may, in reality, be two different brands occupying for example a prestige and premium position in some countries, and a middle market position in others.

About one-third of the promotions we have studied so far have been for European brands, brands which are marketed in many (sometimes all) other European countries, even though the promotion ran only in one country.

Few multinational corporations nowadays lack their European marketing directors or vice presidents. The definition of their range of responsibilities will differ in detail, company by company, as will the nature of these responsibilities *vis-à-vis* their marketing colleagues in individual countries. Some will have 'line' (decision-taking) powers, while others will have only 'staff' (advisory) responsibilities. Either way, what is very likely is that many of them will be spending a lot of time co-ordinating activities such as advertising, media buying, sponsorship and logo/pack/facia design ... and very little time at all on sales promotion matters.

CONSTRAINTS ON PAN-EUROPEAN PROMOTION

How can this be? Why this imbalance? Why should these European marketing directors/vice presidents pay comparatively little attention to an activity on which so large a part of their budgets is spent?

A number of constraints on pan-European promotional activity are commonly suggested – or in some cases concealed. Here is a selection of some of them, starting with one that's often concealed.

PRESERVING NATIONAL MANAGERS' MOTIVATION

It is sometimes felt to be unwise to intervene in sales promotion, for fear of eroding national managers' sense of responsibility, pride and motivation. Let European headquarters confine itself to 'strategic' issues, leaving all 'tactical' matters to managers in individual countries to manage locally.

Sales promotion is identified as a 'tactical' tool, and therefore to be left to local autonomy.

DIFFERENT LANGUAGES, CULTURES, TASTES AND HABITS

The nations of Europe, and the regions within these nations, still have distinct cultural identities.

They speak different languages, and dialects of these languages. They have regional tastes, local sports, distinctive leisure-time activities. It is argued that no single promotion will adequately cater for this diversity.

DIFFERENT LAWS AND REGULATIONS

Equally diverse are the laws and regulations governing sales promotion in different countries. Two tables summarizing what is and is not permitted are given on pages 154 and 155.

At first sight this certainly looks like a minefield through which to navigate a single pan-European promotion!

DIFFERENT PATTERNS OF DISTRIBUTION

Similar products and services are sometimes distributed and retailed through different types of outlets in different European countries. A major brand of toys, for example, may sell primarily through specialist toy shops in the UK, but may have supermarkets as a more important outlet in France.

The promotional requirements of these different types of outlet will differ in important detail.

WHICH COUNTRIES ALLOW WHICH PROMOTION?

	UK	Irish Republic	Spain	West Germany	France	Denmark	Belgium	Netherlands	Portugal	Italy	Greece	Luxembourg
On-pack price reductions	●	●	●	●	●	●	●	●	●	●	●	●
Banded offers	●	●	●	▲	●	▲	▲	●	●	●	●	O
In-pack premiums	●	●	●	▲	▲	▲	▲	▲	●	●	●	O
Multiple-purchase offers	●	●	●	▲	●	▲	▲	●	●	●	●	O
Extra product	●	●	●	▲	●	●	▲	▲	●	●	●	●
Free product	●	●	●	●	●	●	●	●	●	●	●	●
Reusable/alternative use pack	●	●	●	O	●	●	▲	●	●	●	●	●
Free mail-ins	●	●	●	▲	●	▲	▲	▲	●	●	●	▲
With-purchase premiums	●	●	●	O	●	▲	O	▲	●	●	●	O
Cross-product offers	●	●	●	O	●	▲	▲	▲	●	●	●	O
Collector devices	●	●	●	O	▲	▲	▲	▲	●	●	●	▲
Competitions	●	●	●	▲	▲	▲	●	▲	●	●	●	O
Self-liquidating premiums	●	●	●	●	●	●	●	▲	●	●	●	●
Free draws	●	●	●	O	●	O	O	O	●	●	●	O
Share-outs	●	●	●	O	▲	O	O	O	▲	▲	●	O
Sweepstake/lottery	▲	▲	▲	▲	▲	O	▲	▲	●	▲	▲	O
Money-off vouchers	●	●	●	O	●	▲	●	●	●	▲	●	▲
Money-off next purchase	●	●	●	O	●	O	●	●	●	▲	●	O
Cash backs	●	●	●	▲	●	●	●	●	●	O	●	O
In-store demos	●	●	●	●	●	●	●	●	●	●	●	●

● Permitted   O Not permitted   ▲ May be permitted

Table reproduced by kind permission of International Marketing and Promotions

WHICH COUNTRIES ALLOW WHICH PROMOTION?

	UK	Austria	Finland	Norway	Sweden	Switzerland
On-pack price reductions	●	●	●	●	●	●
Banded offers	●	◄	◄	◄	◄	O
In-pack premiums	●	◄	●	◄	◄	O
Multiple-purchase offers	●	◄	◄	◄	◄	O
Extra product	●	◄	●	●	◄	◄
Free product	●	●	●	●	●	●
Reusable/alternative use pack	●	◄	●	●	●	●
Free mail-ins	●	O	●	◄	O	O
With-purchase premiums	●	◄	◄	◄	◄	O
Cross-product offers	●	◄	◄	◄	◄	O
Collector devices	●	O	●	O	O	O
Competitions	●	◄	●	●	●	●
Self-liquidating premiums	●	●	●	O	O	O
Free draws	●	O	●	O	O	O
Share-outs	●	O	◄	◄	O	O
Sweepstake/lottery	◄	◄	●	O	O	O
Money-off vouchers	●	◄	◄	O	◄	O
Money-off next purchase	●	O	◄	O	O	O
Cash backs	●	◄	◄	◄	●	O
In-store demos	●	●	●	●	●	●

● Permitted O Not permitted ◄ May be permitted

Table reproduced by kind permission of International Marketing and Promotions

COMPLEXITY AND RISK

Sales promotions sometimes require very detailed and often complex administration. Many different divisions of the company become involved: marketing; sales; buying and financial departments; production and physical distribution. External suppliers may be involved too, in providing premiums, prizes, advertising for the offer, handling and fulfilment, merchandising etc.

In such complex operations the risk of something going wrong is ever present. One weak link can break the chain. Every promotion can prove a fiasco. Close supervision and hands-on management is vital to ensure success.

Few European headquarters are staffed to provide such close supervision. And many European marketing vice presidents decide that co-ordination of sales promotion would be 'a can of worms' – best left unopened.

NONE THE LESS!

A number of current developments, notably the creation of the European 'single market', put a question mark against some of these traditional assumptions and practices.

Rather than argue the case in the abstract, however, let's look first at some actual promotions which have run across national boundaries in Europe, that have been at least part- if not quite pan-European.

At a political and governmental level much current discussion of the 'new' Europe is clouded on the one hand by philosophical abstraction, idealism and Utopianism, and on the other by vested interests, prejudice and historical hang-ups. Within corporations much the same forces are at work in discussions of European branding, marketing, advertising and sales promotion.

A study of actual cases helps discipline the discussion.

CARDHU CREAM TRUFFLES

BACKGROUND

Johnnie Walker 'Cardhu' is a single malt whisky, from the distillery of that name in the Glens of Strathspey, Scotland. There it is matured for 12 years, before being put in a notably elegant and distinctive bottle.

Whisky has been distilled at Cardhu since 1824. Today it is marketed world-wide by the United Distillers Group, which in 1987 established a specialist division to optimize the performance of its portfolio of brands in duty-free outlets.

Scotch whisky is a favourite duty-free 'buy' of international travellers, and competition between brands is intense to increase share of this large-volume market. Cardhu was identified as having excellent potential for further growth in duty-free outlets, and was given a high priority for promotional support. The evidence indicated that sales could be increased sharply if Cardhu was brought strongly to the attention of potential consumers.

THE PROMOTION

Well-groomed personality girls in tartan outfits circulated in the international departure lounges of airports, carrying silver salvers bearing individual cream truffles. Passengers were invited to try one, and the girls explained that a presentation box of these handmade truffles was being offered as a gift with a purchase of Cardhu in the adjacent duty-free shop.

The promotion was mounted, usually for four-week periods, in airports at Heathrow, Gatwick, Geneva, Rome, Madrid and Nice during 1988.

Results

Weekly sales of Cardhu increased by an average of 1000 per cent as a result of the promotion.

The promotion was subsequently extended to other airports.

Agency: Clarke Hooper

Cream truffles, a gift from Johnnie Walker Cardhu whisky in airport duty free shops round Europe

COMMENT

International promotions – crossing national boundaries – have perhaps developed faster in duty-free outlets than in other trade sectors. After all, duty-free shops cater for an international public, for travellers crossing national boundaries themselves.

This very elegant promotion gets a big tick against every criterion of judgement. Its elegance is itself right for a premium brand. The fact that the truffles are handmade reflects the traditional skills that have gone into the distilling and maturing of the whisky.

The truffles are perfect for offering, individually, as a highly acceptable sample to travellers waiting in a departure lounge. This was something personality girls could offer with confidence (not always the case with some promotional offers with which the public is accosted).

Boxed, the truffles make a perfect small gift for a secretary or wife – the businessman's own if he's heading for home and buying the whisky for himself, or maybe his host's wife or secretary if he's on an outward journey, the host getting the Cardhu. Or, then again, the traveller can self-indulgently eat the truffles himself, or herself – no one at the other end will be any the wiser, since the box is quite separate from the bottle, and the bottle carries no reference to it.

There is a big tick too from the duty-free shop manager: this promotion brought some passengers into the shop who might otherwise have stayed outside in the departure lounge.

STANLEY HELP THE RED CROSS BUILD A BETTER WORLD

BACKGROUND

Stanley Tools is the leading brand in the hand tool market in Europe. The maintenance of this position against stiff competition from other branded or own-label products is an on-going task.

In 1991 Stanley sought a promotion capable of assisting selling-in and stocking of their range of tools, justifying display and stimulating consumer sales.

The promotion needed to be compatible in theme and style with Stanley's leading role in the sector, and had to reinforce the brand image at point of purchase. Some element of innovation would gain extra attention. And to add to the promotion's scale and importance a common Europe-wide solution was preferred to what was essentially a common European requirement.

This charity promotion ran in 11 European countries in 1991

THE PROMOTION

The European public was invited to 'Help the Red Cross Build a Better World' when they purchased Stanley Tools.

A percentage of the net sales value of promotional stock sold to the trade was donated by Stanley to a Red Cross 'tool fund'.

As the fund started to grow a credit line was opened for Red Cross enabling it to draw tools direct from Stanley warehouses across Europe for immediate disaster relief. Also pre-packed kits continue to be supplied to the Red Cross's own stores. They are

- an Emergency Kit containing basic equipment for disaster relief;
- a Mechanical Kit for vehicle and vital machinery maintenance; and
- a Construction Kit for rebuilding shelters and field hospitals, and maintaining supplies of vital amenities.

The programme was designed for maximum flexibility, to ensure that the tools get to the people who need them quickly.

The promotion was communicated at the point of purchase by floor-standing display cases and shelf trays, pre-packed with tools and with header cards carrying the 'Help Stanley Help the Red Cross Build a Better World' message.

The promotion was mounted in the UK, Eire, France, Holland, Belgium, Spain, Italy, Denmark, Sweden, Norway and Finland.

Individual countries made individual consumer offers. In the UK cash refunds of between £1 and £3 were offered on promoted tools, with the consumer having the option of instructing Stanley instead to double the cash sum and donate additional tools to that value to the Red Cross.

This cash-back offer was replicated in many other countries, with varying values of cash refunded, but in Scandinavia the cash back was dropped in favour of simply asking consumers to send in proofs of purchase to help Stanley further build the tool fund.

Results

The promotion received an enthusiastic welcome from the distributive trade and Stanley sales forces across Europe. Stocking and presentation of the Stanley range improved and special in-store displays were achieved in many outlets.

Despite very depressed market conditions the promotion generated a tool fund for the Red Cross of approximately US$600,000 worth of tools.

Agency: AM-C (now FSC)

COMMENT

The promotion provided a perfect bridge between Stanley and the Red Cross, both helping to build a better world in their own way. The link was also relevant and credible: the Red Cross having a genuine need for tools in their daily activity.

This was the first such link the International Red Cross had made with a commercial organization. Indeed, this seems to be the first time that a promotional tie-up with any charity has run on such a wide, pan-European scale.

The negotiations with the Red Cross were complex. Not only did they involve top-level negotiation in Geneva where a formal contract had to be agreed, but they also included national negotiations with individual governments. The words 'Red Cross' and the Red Cross emblem are protected under the Geneva convention, and in the UK, for example, written permission had to be obtained from both the Department of Trade and Industry and the Ministry of Defence.

THE INTERNATIONAL SWATCH COLLECTORS' CLUB

BACKGROUND

Swatch watches were launched in 1983 by the large Swiss group, SMH, which already produced Longines, Omega, Tissot and Rado. Swatch was SMH's entry in the new quartz sector, pioneered by the Japanese.

At first Swatch watches were of conventional design, but in 1984 more radical models were introduced, with increasingly unusual designs being featured in two fashion collections a year. Sales started to soar immediately: despite typically Swiss high standards of quality these new watches were inexpensive, and they rapidly established themselves as one of the most chic but most affordable collections around. Many fashion-conscious teenagers in Europe, Japan and the USA own at least three Swatches, and there are even Swatch 'freaks' with more than a thousand Swatches!

Demand has frequently exceeded supply and even standard production models often resell at a premium soon after their appearance. Some special limited editions have commanded prices of up to £20,000. Prototypes can cost even more.

As the 1980s drew to a close Swatch sought a promotional vehicle that would consolidate and build on this enormous commercial success. This was a scheme that would put Swatch in closer contact with its fans, while at the same time offering strong support to that relatively small number of retailers through whom most Swatch sales were made.

As Swatch was already an international phenomenon there was never any doubt that this needed to be an international scheme.

THE PROMOTION

The public was invited to join 'The International Swatch Collectors' Club'. Annual membership cost approximately £50.

Membership of the club was confirmed by a certificate, and each year the member received:

- a limited edition Swatch, available only to members;
- two issues of the *Swatch Street Journal*;

The Swatch Collectors' Club is international just like the watches themselves

- advance information about new product introductions;
- information about Swatch auctions;
- a magazine dedicated to buying and selling or trading old Swatches between members;
- invitations to Swatch nights out, weekends, activity holidays;
- and a surprise mailing.

Members were recruited by a PR programme, and by advertising and leaflets at the point of purchase.

The database was made available to key retailers for their own additional local mailings.

The International Swatch Collectors' Club was launched first in Switzerland and Germany in August 1989; in Italy in January 1990; in France and Austria in August 1991; in Spain and the UK in August 1992.

Results

Already by mid 1992 in excess of 100,000 members had joined the club.

Agency: RSCG International

COMMENT

The modest cost of membership now covers the expense of this promotion as a result of the great economies produced by holding the database internationally, while updating it locally.

WIN A GHOST IN A CAN

BACKGROUND

Coca-Cola is served in all Burger King outlets, throughout Europe. Young people are a key target market for Burger King, and for its fast food competitors. They are big fans of Coca-Cola too. They also fill most seats in the local cinema, and much of Hollywood's movie output is directed at children and young adults.

Ghostbusters achieved an enormous box office success with this young audience. Coca-Cola and Burger King combined in the following promotion, designed to exploit interest in Ghostbusters II *as this follow-up film was released across Europe in 1989.*

THE PROMOTION

Young people visiting Burger King restaurants were invited to 'Win a Ghost in a Can'. The 'Ghost Licence' issued with the can explained the concept:

> This is to certify that the holder of this licence is the owner of a genuine vanishing ghost, captured and en-can-sulated by Ghostbuster.
>
> Your ghost will be safe and happy in this can – but under no circumstances should he be released!
>
> WARNING! Should this can be accidentally opened or the seal broken your ghost will immediately escape into thin air and vanish forever.
>
> However, if you expose the can to strong light for a few minutes and then take it into a dark room, a ghostly green afterglow will appear inside the can.
>
> I hereby promise to keep my ghost safe and happy.
>
> Signed _____

Winning the can involved exercising skill and judgement in deciding which latex panels to rub off on *Ghostbusters II* game cards issued in the restaurants. These cards also gave opportunities to win a cup of Coke.

The promotion ran in seven countries across Europe: the UK; Ireland; Germany; France; Spain; Italy; and Holland.

Local laws were closely observed in the detailing of the competition. For example, in Germany the game cards were available by writing in as an alternative to visiting a Burger King.

GHOST LICENCE

This is to certify that the holder of this licence is the owner of a genuine vanishing ghost, captured and en-can-sulated by Ghostbusters.

Your ghost will be safe and happy in this can – but under no circumstances should he be released!

See Ghostbusters II at a cinema near you.

WARNING! Should this can be accidentally opened or the seal broken your ghost will immediately escape into thin air and vanish forever. However, if you expose the can to strong light for a few minutes and then take it into a dark room, a ghostly green afterglow will appear inside the can.

I hereby promise to keep my ghost safe and happy.

Signed _____

NB. If opened, do not fill and drink from this can. 'Coca-Cola' and 'Coke' are registered trade marks which identify the same product of The Coca-Cola Company. © Burger King Corporation USA.

Coca-Cola, Ghostbusters II *and Burger King – working together in this 'Ghost in a Can' promotion in seven European countries*

Results

Traffic was up and increases were reported in Coca-Cola volume.

Agency: IMP

COMMENT

Capturing a ghost in a can is an amusing idea in its own right and for Coca-Cola it was a totally relevant use of a merchandising licence. Solving the challenges posed by the *Ghostbuster* game cards added to the fun of visiting Burger King with friends. And the chance to win a Coke contributed the serious reward element in a very entertaining promotion.

All three 'partners', Burger King, Coca-Cola and the *Ghostbusters* film had an international following. To have run such a promotion in just one European country would have been a waste of a first-class promotional concept.

THE SCOTCH VIDEOCASSETTES BOOK OF THE OLYMPICS

BACKGROUND

By 1983, 3M had built a strong position in the fast-growing European market for blank videocassettes with its Scotch brand. The year 1984 was an Olympics year, and the Olympics looked a promising theme for promoting the brand. All past evidence indicated that major sporting events, when shown on television, produced a surge in sales: sports enthusiasts buying an extra videocassette to record the event for playback, especially if they were not going to be near their television sets when the live event was broadcast.

The Olympics, with their many events, justified buying a couple of extra cassettes, or more. The fact that the Games were being held in Los Angeles, on the west coast of America, implied that with the several hours' time difference from Europe many of the most popular events would be taking place when all good Europeans would be in bed. European videorecording was thus likely to peak sharply.

The promotional opportunity seemed too important to leave to individual 3M managements in individual countries to develop their own exploitation of the Olympics. At the very least it would be wastefully time-consuming to have a dozen different marketing departments working perhaps with a dozen different sales promotion agencies, each coming up with their own different ideas (sometimes with the same ideas perhaps), and each country then buying in whatever print or premium materials were required to implement the chosen ideas.

The company's European marketing headquarters, in Brussels, therefore decided to take a central initiative, and to develop a pan-European Olympics promotion.

THE PROMOTION

Scotch videocassettes offered a *Scotch Book of the Olympics*, to act as a guide and a companion to the European television viewer. The book contained comprehensive facts about the Olympics, their history,

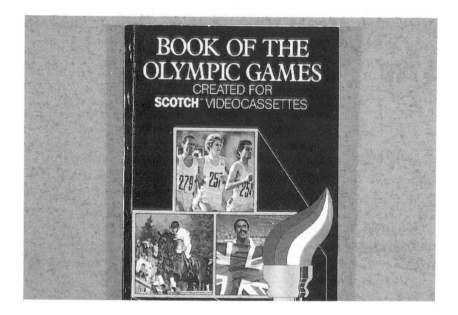

The cover of the British edition pictured middle distance running, an equestrian event and the decathlon – all sports in which Britain excelled

current records in the various events, the Los Angeles programme of events, leading athletes likely to reach the finals of their sports and so forth. Most of this factual or quasi-factual information was non-contentious, that is, not subject to nationalistic or partisan bias.

However, since the Olympic competitions are in fact an occasion for competition between the nations, arousing considerable patriotic fervour, part of the book was left available for individual countries' particular interests in the Los Angeles events. National 3M managers were consulted on what their own countries' interests were for this section. The point was visually illustrated on the covers: the covers of all the various national editions had an identical format, but the spaces occupied by the three large action pictures were filled with different photographs.

Thus, the British cover featured middle-distance running, the decathalon and an equestrian event, these being competitions in which the British had strong medal prospects in Los Angeles.

The plan was to make the promotion's impact as heavy as possible by offering the book free with the purchase of two Scotch videocassettes. To keep within the available budgets this pointed to a paperback, rather than hardback format, but with full-colour illustrations throughout. Moreover, it was necessary to keep within the legal requirement of some European countries that a free premium should not exceed in cost a certain specified percentage of the price of the brand offering the premium.

The production costs of the book were further minimized by obtaining quotations for printing it from a large number of candidate suppliers in several European countries. The contract for printing all the books for all participating countries, in 12 different languages, was finally awarded to a single Spanish printer. The books were delivered to the 3M video-cassette production plant in Wales, where for most countries they were banded to two Scotch cassettes prior to shipping.

Throughout the whole development and implementation of of this promotion 3M national managers were closely consulted. A range of possible ideas was sketched out for exploiting this consumer promotion, the book, in trade terms, but national managers were left entirely free to use one of these trade ideas or to develop their own.

Results

3M's share of the blank videocassette markets advanced throughout Europe during this promotion.

Agency: The Sales Machine International

COMMENT

This case study illustrates a multinational corporation choosing its moment – the surge in demand about to be created by the Olympics – to develop a pan-European promotion that was more ambitious than might reasonably have been attempted by individual countries. Individual countries might well have been deterred by the time, effort and expense required to employ and supervise the necessary team of sports journalists, picture editors, designers, finished artists and printers. As it was, the promotional premium, the book, catered for national dif-ferences, while national managers were also left free to decide how best to handle those aspects of the promotion (in this case trade exploitation) which they knew much more about in their own countries than did 3M's European HQ.

Note that this promotion dates back to 1984, to illustrate that there was nothing new, visionary or impractical about running promotions across national boundaries, in Europe, even before the introduction of the 'single market'.

The same concept, local variations, for this Scotch videocassette pan-European promotion

10

THE WAY AHEAD

SALES PROMOTION IN A SINGLE COUNTRY

In every European country significant shares of many business sectors are still controlled by companies indigenous to that country, operating only in that one country, or at least making the overwhelming majority of their sales within their domestic market. For such companies, by definition, sales promotion will remain a single country activity. Any export sales will usually be stripped of promotions created for the domestic market to avoid linguistic and administrative confusion.

A number of multinational companies, too, own certain brands which are marketed only in a single European country. Again, promotions for these brands will, of course, be designed for one country only.

Other multinationals who own pan-European brands (or at least brands marketed in several European countries) will none the less remain wedded to the philosophy that sales promotions are best created and implemented by national managements in individual countries.

There seems little doubt, too, that many distinct national tastes, interests and habits will persist well into the 21st century, if not beyond. The English will continue to play cricket and the Spaniards no doubt to fight bulls. Germans and Italians show little sign of following their example.

No matter: for certain brands, marketed only in England or Spain, cricket and bullfighting may well form relevant and motivating themes for sales promotion, and these brands will be in position to exploit them strongly without the distraction of having to worry about what to do instead in other countries.

Even international brands, originating from outside England or Spain, may decide on occasion to run promotions in these countries based on these sports. Perhaps they may wish to communicate and emphasize what good 'local citizens' they are, how well domiciled they are in their hosts' countries and how well attuned to the local lifestyle.

SALES PROMOTION ACROSS NATIONAL BOUNDARIES

There seems equally little doubt, however, that we shall see an ever-increasing number of promotions running across national boundaries in Europe. We have studied examples in Chapter 9, and there are sure to be more in subsequent editions of this book.

Here are some of the reasons why.

THE EUROPEAN SINGLE MARKET

The advent of the 'single market' within the EC, and the inclusion of European Free Trade Association countries within many of its arrangements, greatly facilitates the buying of goods and services in one country for sale in another.

Sales promotions 'attached to' a brand in one country will increasingly spill over into other European countries.

Corporations managed only on a traditional country-by-country basis will be ill equipped to control, let alone exploit, this development. This is especially so in business sectors where wholesale and retail distributors themselves begin to operate internationally, making acquisitions or forming consortia across national boundaries.

COMMUNICATION MEDIA

A growing number of – especially broadcast – media now span more than one country. On occasion they will represent cost-effective channels for the communication of sales promotional messages, to a particular type of audience, at a particular time, in a particular editorial context. Such media will effectively be denied to – or messages will be wasted by – companies planning their sales promotion activities exclusively within single countries.

ECONOMIES OF SCALE

Most sales promotions involve the promoter in buying goods and/or services from external suppliers. The list of possible requirements may include creative concept services, from a sales promotion agency/

consultancy; design, photography, finished artwork; printing; premiums; prizes; advertising support; handling and fulfilment; rights to patented or copyright goods or services etc.

The unit cost of many of these is reduced when the volume is greater. Similarly, 'capital' costs (eg creative services of all types) are more easily affordable when amortized across a large volume. So, mounting the same promotion in more than one country increases volumes while reducing unit costs.

EFFICIENT USE OF MANAGEMENT TIME

Sales promotions require considerable management time to be devoted to them, both in development and implementation. Small, low-budget promotions often require as much management attention as big promotions. In some companies, on some brands, junior members of marketing departments may spend more than half their working time on sales promotional matters. Management time can represent an expensive (but usually hidden) on-cost on promotional budgets.

Promotions which are used in more than one country, and which avoid country-by-country duplication of this effort, will improve the efficiency with which management time is deployed.

Much time is still wasted by managers in individual countries 'reinventing the wheel' – starting out from closely similar promotional requirements to arrive at answers closely similar to those already developed by a colleague in another country a year earlier.

EXPLOITATION OF EXCELLENCE

Worse still is when this duplication of effort results in less effective promotions in some countries than another, when the solutions arrived at independently are different, when one is much better than all the others, but the less effective solutions are none the less employed in the countries which developed them.

Relevant, powerful, unique promotional concepts are rare. In fact they are as rare as 'great' advertising campaigns. Much month-by-month promotional activity is frankly pedestrian.

A brand fortunate enough to have a relevant, powerful and unique concept has an asset worth its weight in gold – deserving a place in the company's financial balance sheet.

Sometimes such powerful concepts are stumbled upon almost by accident. They may arise as a by-product of other work being done on advertising development, pack design, trade motivation programmes, merchandising – or whatever. Their effectiveness, the results they achieve, may surprise and even astonish the managers responsible.

To leave such a concept lying where it was found is as crass as stumbling over the world's biggest diamond and noting only that it scratched your boot. There is no excuse for seeing a promotion developed for Carrefour hypermarkets in France quadruple the brand's sales, and yet failing to examine the possibility of adapting it and extending it to the rest of the French trade, and maybe for the rest of Europe too.

More often such rare, 'great' concepts are the result of systematic and painstaking development by the best 'brains' in the business. However widely diffused understanding of sales promotion is now, compared with 25 years ago, *outstanding* talent is still scarce. It may be found in just one or two of the national managements of a European multinational; one of the sales promotion agencies national managements use is likely to be better at this creative concept work than others.

Wherever excellence is to be found, by accident or design, it needs to be exploited on the widest possible geographic scale.

CONSISTENCY OF BRAND MESSAGES

All forms of marketing support, all marketing expenditures, communicate messages about the brand. Advertising typically takes the main responsibility for communicating the central brand proposition, for putting across the brand's fundamental characteristics, qualities and competitive benefits. Sales promotion more often communicates additional, subsidiary benefits; for example, a special offer.

What the audience receives from these various messages is an overall impression of the brand. People in the audience are unlikely to distinguish between advertising and sales promotion messages in the same sophisticated way as the marketing people who designed them. Consumers cannot be expected to prioritize what the advertising says to them as 'important', but what the sales promotion offers as 'less important'. They will draw inferences about the brand from both sources, especially as advertisements are usually separated from the brand, appearing on television, billboards, radio or in newspapers and magazines, whereas sales promotions are often physically attached to the brand, appearing on fmcg packs or in the windows of retailers promoting their stores. Consumers reading a promotional offer on the back of a cereal pack over breakfast are likely to assume that this is the brand telling them something about itself, in just the same way as it was telling them something in the television commercial they may (or may not) have seen the previous evening. The back-of-pack message gets through to most buyers or consumers of the breakfast cereal; only very large budget advertising campaigns will reach so many.

Consistency in all these various messages, both advertising and sales promotional, is therefore vital if consumers are to end up with a coherent understanding of what the brand is, how it is compatible with their own personality and why it is the right choice for them. Sales promotions will confuse and damage consumers' perceptions of the brand if they have themes inconsistent with the brand's personality, if they offer goods or services of different quality from that of the brand itself, if they are implemented and administered to lower standards of performance than the brand itself delivers. Such promotions can only detract from the favourable attitudes so carefully cultivated by advertising and other brand-enhancing activities, such as public relations and product development.

If this seems uncontentious – commonly accepted wisdom – more contentious in some marketing circles is what can be argued to be a logical conclusion. This is that if a European headquarters sees one of its key responsibilities to be to act as the ultimate guardian of a brand's personality, its positioning *vis-à-vis* competitors and its basic values, then it needs to take a view on the character of the messages about the brand being pumped out by sales promotions.

This is particularly so if the amount of money spent on these promotions forms a significant proportion of the total budgets deployed in support of the brand.

STRATEGY, TACTICS AND SUBSIDIARITY

All these considerations point to an important role for European headquarters in overseeing the development of promotional concepts, as part of their strategic responsibilities for their brands' positioning, for communicating their brands' values.

Tactical exploitation and implementation of these concepts will, in principle, remain the responsibility of national managements. But the dividing line between strategy and tactics often becomes blurred in promotional practice; it is likely to shift position from one type of promotion to another.

A better operating principle is that of 'subsidiarity', which is at the heart of so much discussion about the location of political and economic power within the EC. To paraphrase the wording of a draft treaty of union from 1984:

European headquarters shall only act to carry out those tasks which may be undertaken more effectively in common than by national managements acting separately, in particular those whose execution requires action by European headquarters because their dimension or effects extend beyond national boundaries.

Thus, an identical promotional prize for all countries will most economically be sourced centrally. Telephone-answering services to handle entries by consumers competing to win these prizes will clearly be best set up locally – international phone calls would merely introduce diseconomies.

NEW SKILLS AND OPERATING PROCEDURES

Creating relevant and effective concepts for sales promotions designed to run across national boundaries makes subtly different demands from working within a single country's boundaries. New skills and new types of expertise will need to be developed by those involved.

Companies owning European brands will need modified operating procedures to manage these international promotions. Some job specifications will need rewriting, both at headquarters and in individual countries.

Sales promotion agencies will have to decide whether to equip themselves to handle pan-European requirements, or whether to concentrate only on domestic business instead. Many American agencies thrive and prosper by working in just one state or region of the US. Equally, there's no reason why European agencies should not continue to succeed commercially within the confines of a single country, given that single country promotions will continue to account for a large part of even multinational clients' spending for the foreseeable future. Nor will a decision to compete for European promotional work necessarily require the setting up of a network of offices in every European country. Some multinational clients will require only concept creation from their chosen agency, preferring the exploitation and tactical implementation of these concepts to be handled by their national managements, these managements employing whatever local external services they choose. Clearly, however, the agency will need knowledge, understanding and 'feel' for the countries involved to be able to create concepts which are right for them.

AUDITING

The number and diversity of sales promotions mounted by a European brand in different countries – the volume and complexity of the administration they require – has often deterred European headquarters from intervening. It's difficult to know where to start!

The first step will often be simply to establish the current facts, to gain a clear picture of what's being done, and why, and with what results. This will be done by conducting an 'audit' of the brand's recent sales promotions across Europe.

The scope of such an audit will depend on the particular circumstances of the brand and the nature of its marketing mix, but the following questions are typical of those a fmcg audit will set out to answer.

- What total sums of money are being spent below-the-line in each of the countries to be audited? What percentages of total marketing support budgets do they represent? In particular, how do they relate in size to expenditures on advertising? What percentages of sales revenues are these below-the-line budgets?

- What are the break-downs between trade- and consumer-directed promotional spends?

- What are the objectives trade promotions are designed to achieve:
  — holding/widening distribution?
  — supporting/increasing volume/stock levels?
  — in-store display?
  — other objectives?

- What are the promotional techniques being used to achieve these trade objectives:
  — discounts off trade prices?
  — more for the same price?
  — annual volume discounts?
  — payments for display?
  — gifts for the trade?
  — other techniques?

- What percentages of trade expenditure are being spent on each objective, each technique?

- Which trade channels are getting what shares of expenditure? How do these shares of expenditure equate to the shares of sales accounted for by these different trade channels?

- What are the objectives of consumer promotions:
  — consumer trial/retrial?
  — consumer loyalty?
  — favourable influencing of consumer attitudes?
  — other objectives?

- What promotional techniques are being used to achieve these consumer objectives:
  - retail price reductions? (In which forms?)
  - free samples? (How distributed?)
  - coupons? (How distributed?)
  - free premiums? (With what purchase requirements?)
  - self-liquidating premiums?
  - prize promotions?
  - promotional games?
  - other techniques?

- What percentages of consumer promotion budgets are being spent against each objective, each technique?

Answering these and similar questions involves little more, in the first instance, than collecting facts. Many of these can be gleaned from the individual countries' annual marketing plans, plus an examination of planning papers for promotional activities.

A more qualitative element is introduced into the audit when the factual answer to each question is subjected to the further question *Why?* What was the rationale behind each of these many decisions: how much to spend, against these target audiences, to achieve these objectives, employing these techniques?

Some element of judgement will similarly be needed as the audit moves on to question the *results* of all these promotional activities. A mature evaluation of even sales promotions can rarely rely only on statistical data. And, alas, it's only a minority of companies which consistently evaluates and reports on the results of all their promotions.

It's at this point that the benefits of a European audit begin to show through. The evaluation of a promotion in one country is in an important sense incomplete, unless its cost and effectiveness has been compared with the cost and effectiveness of promotions for the same brand in other countries – promotions that were attempting to achieve the same objective.

For example, the management in country A may congratulate itself on achieving the 200,000 trialists set as an objective for a promotion, within the budgeted cost of $2.50 each. The management may be particularly pleased, since alternative promotional techniques for inducing trial have in the past cost over $3.00 per trialist. But what if the international audit indicates that the average cost per trialist for the brand in seven other countries which the audit has grouped with country A is only $1.50 – this grouping having been based on the brand being, for example, at a similar stage of development? It's at least worth looking to see what these promotions are that have achieved an apparently more cost-effective inducing of trial in other countries in the group. It may be especially worth looking at country B, which has consistently spent no more than $1.00 to gain a trialist, using a technique which interestingly enough, hasn't been used in quite that form by any other country. There may be something to be learned from country B, maybe even imitated. Of course, special factors may apply in country B, but even so it may still be possible to discount these. Or perhaps this promotional technique which country B is using so successfully is not legal in some of the other countries in the group. Maybe not, but let's see: differences in law between different countries are not a problem until they become a problem in specific instances.

Similar benchmarks of effectiveness are likely to emerge for all common objectives and for all techniques employed, as the audit data is subject to experienced and sensitive analysis. Notable successes in individual countries will begin to show up more clearly than ever before against this tabulated background of other countries' experience. Underperformance will be shown as such.

Presented with this data, other more sophisticated analyses will be possible. For example, it may be very illuminating to differentiate across all markets between promotions that clearly communicate the brand's position and those that don't. And to reclassify with advertising expenditure those promotions which enhance understanding of the brand and encourage favourable attitudes towards it. Clearly, subjective judgement will be involved in making this differentiation, but it's precisely this type of judgement that European headquarters, in their role as guardians of their brands' distinctive values, should be well equipped to make.

In most corporations this audit of sales promotions will best be conducted in close consultation with managements in the countries to be audited. Conclusions derived from the audit should be arrived at and agreed with these managements. The minimum use to which these findings should be put should be a mutual learning process, designed to encourage successful promotional activities and to weed out failures, now that successes and failures have been much more clearly identified. Areas of common endeavour, perhaps areas where major problems are being encountered, may be candidates for new promotional initiatives to be orchestrated from the centre, using the most expert promotional resources available in Europe, whose location may well have been identified by the audit.

EMERGENCE OF COMMON EUROPEAN INTERESTS

The feasibility of running single sales promotions across national boundaries is increased by the emergence of a growing number of interests, tastes and activities which the peoples of Europe have in common.
Here's a short list of just some of them.

SPORTING EVENTS:

- the European Cup and World Cup soccer competitions;
- the Olympic Games;
- Wimbledon and other 'Grand Slam' tennis tournaments;
- Grand Prix motor racing.

MUSIC:

- leading pop groups;
- the Eurovision Song Contest;
- festivals in Salzburg and Bayreuth.

TRAVEL AND TRANSPORT:

- vacations in other European countries;
- Concorde;
- New York, San Francisco and Hollywood;
- luxury cars like Mercedes, BMWs and Jaguars;
- Avis, Hertz and other car rentals.

TELEVISION:

- *Dallas*;
- *Dynasty*;
- *Kojak.*

CHILDREN'S INTERESTS:

- space travel;
- animals;
- dolls;
- pirates and buried treasure;

- LEGO toys;
- Disney.

FASHION:

- Levis;
- Benetton;
- Gucci.

FINANCIAL SERVICES:

- American Express, Visa, Mastercard;
- Europ Assistance.

SOCIAL CONCERN:

- Red Cross;
- World Wide Fund for Nature;
- the environment;
- starvation relief;
- drug abuse.

These and many others are available as common currency for Europe-wide sales promotional themes. We have seen some of them being put to good use already by, for example, Scotch videocassettes and Stanley Tools, in Chapter 9.

Many of them are minority interests, but so are even the most successful brands. Even brand leaders rarely account for as much as 50 per cent of the sales in their sectors, and the majority of well-known and profitable brands achieve market shares of only between 15 per cent and 33 per cent.

Successful European brands succeed in practice by appealing to like-minded minorities in different countries. These minorities will have other interests in common, in parallel to their preference for these brands.

AVOIDING BLANDNESS

There is a danger to be avoided, however. This is that a desire to co-ordinate and align promotional themes can go too far, resulting in promotions that are bland and generalized, rather than sharp and specific; themes that represent the lowest common denominator of pan-European tastes, rather than the highest common factor in the brand's unique appeal.

The underlying objective of creating a single promotion for a number of different countries needs to be kept clearly in mind: it is to equip each individual country with a better, more effective, less costly, perhaps more ambitious promotion than it could readily have achieved from its own resources.

Persuading a country to participate in a pan-European promotion can be counter-productive if the promotion is clearly less relevant in that country than in others. Skiing remains a minority sport in the UK, and a promotion based on skiing will have a much narrower appeal in the UK than in many continental European countries. If wide appeal is necessary to the success of the promotion, the UK company will be better left to pursue its own separate promotion.

LEGISLATORS AND REGULATORS

The diversity of laws and regulations governing sales promotional activities in different European countries undoubtedly represents a barrier to the deployment of the same promotions across national frontiers. Even though we have studied cases where this barrier has been overcome, harmonization of these rules would undoubtedly hasten the creation of a single market for sales promotions.

Unfortunately, all too many of the precedents set by the European Commission in harmonizing the framework within which other business activities are conducted in the EC suggest that such harmonization might well result in a more restrictive regime which could be based, for example, on the severe restrictions currently in force in Germany, rather than on the more liberal regimes that operate in Spain or the UK.

The case for such restrictions seems weak. Presumably such restrictions are based on a wish to protect consumers from misleading or 'unfair' promotional practices and from the abuse of monopolistic power by dominant suppliers.

No supporter of free markets (which must include everybody who has chosen to work in sales promotion) wishes to see monopolies. However, the European Commission has been assuming stronger powers to check the formation of such monopolies (eg by merger or acquisition) everywhere within the EC, and there seems little case therefore for restricting the promotional activities of companies competing openly in non-monopolistic markets. On the contrary, restrictions on sales promotion will represent a barrier to new competitors attempting to enter such markets, limiting their ability to attack established suppliers with the type of launch promotions we studied for example in Chapters 2 and 3. Consumer choice will be restricted as a result.

Nor does any professional sales promotion practitioner wish consciously to mislead consumers about the nature, value or terms of any offer. Instances where the communication of offers may be construed as potentially misleading are rare in relation to the very large number of new promotions which appear every week throughout the year. Complaints to regulatory bodies are correspondingly few. Moreover, they usually result from unclear or incomplete copy rather than from any intention to deceive. And most often they thereby carelessly infringe voluntary codes of conduct, close observance of which eliminates the vast majority of potentially misleading descriptions.

Of course there are always a few sales promoters who are not professional, who do not behave reputably and who will wantonly ignore voluntary codes of conduct. They are to be found, however, in businesses which are themselves disreputable, and which governmental and legal bodies will act to discipline as businesses, rather than as users of sales promotions. It is heavy-handed and inappropriate to frame laws which impede free and open trading by the many, in an attempt to clamp down on the abuses of 0.1 per cent!

There remains the view that some types of sales promotion are 'unfair'. This introduces a highly subjective element into regulation. A typical argument is that 'too generous' an offer will place undue pressure on the consumer to buy the product or service promoted, in preference to that of an unpromoted competitor, and that therefore, for example, a limit must be placed on the value of any free gift in relation to the cost of the purchase necessary to obtain it. Such an argument shows little faith in the commercial acumen of the businesspeople making the offer, who have presumably calculated that the cost of the free gift is affordable in terms of the additional sales it is designed to stimulate – calculations which themselves will limit the generosity of the gift. What concern is it of legislators and regulators if the calculation is wrong, if the promoter suffers loss as a result of being over-generous? Such losses can occur equally from businesses miscalculating prices in relation to volumes. In all cases the consumer benefits at the supplier's expense. Is that such a bad outcome? Such arguments, leading to restrictions, also evidence considerable contempt for consumers' intelligence, for their ability to make rational and discriminating purchase decisions. Perhaps a century or more ago there may have been a case for protecting European consumers against their own fecklessness in this way, but in the 1990s businesses receive daily evidence that they are selling to a well-educated, well-informed and very sophisticated public.

This over-protective, paternalistic attitude on the part of legislators and regulators can be seen at work even in countries which are comparatively 'permissive' in respect of sales promotion activities. In the UK, for example, it is illegal to require the purchase of a promoted product or service as a qualification for competing to win a prize, if winners are to be determined by 'lot' or 'chance' (eg by drawing winners' names out of a hat). The original legislation dates back to the nineteenth century when it was feared that poor and uneducated people might be tempted to purchase a luxury they could ill afford, in the naïve expectation of winning a prize – the odds against which they were ill equipped to understand. The legislation has been re-enacted in the recent past, with essentially the same restrictive effect on prize promotions, even though it is difficult to imagine children in late twentieth century Britain going hungry to bed or shoeless to school because their parents were foolish enough to squander their last pound on some inessential, in order to enter for a £1,000 lottery prize. Such lotteries, requiring the purchase of the promoted product or service, are permitted in Italy, for example, and there is no evidence of Italian consumers coming to any harm as a result.

Sales promoters throughout Europe will have justice, common sense, and the cause of free and prosperous markets on their side if they resist strongly the imposition of further restrictions on their activities, and if they fight fiercely for the removal of most current legal restraints.

In many countries voluntary codes of conduct, policed by the industry itself, provide an entirely adequate protection against abuses. European sales promoters have now agreed a common code; they need to propose effective means of ensuring it is observed; and thus to provide the European Commission with the text for new and more rational European regulations, to supersede all existing national laws and restrictions.

Appendix B contains a proposed outline of such European regulations.

A Footnote on Eastern Europe and the Commonwealth of Independent States (CIS)

By Karen May

Introduction

We have been witnessing throughout the whole of Eastern Europe dramatic changes in both political and economic structure. The removal of the Berlin Wall, the overthrow of Ceauşescu and the breaking up of the Soviet Union into independent Republics, to highlight but a few events, have marked the rejection of the Communist old guard by its peoples. However, the metamorphosis is not yet complete and unfortunately it is likely that such economies will continue to get worse before they get better. What is undeniable though, is that the East's move away from the Communist system will eventually open up its respective markets further to Western companies. Prospects for the penetration of Western goods, and the adoption of Western marketing skills on a large scale, are very much in the future, though they could prove to be extremely lucrative.

Eastern Europe and the former Soviet Union offer a potential customer base of 425 million consumers. Companies with their hearts set on making inroads into the region need to have money, commitment and long term-vision. The UK Department of Trade and Industry recommends that only large well-established companies which can afford to cover their losses should actively seek involvement.

Opportunities for export did, of course, exist under the old regime. Trade with the CIS, for example, was conducted via FTOs – its 100 foreign trade associations. In many ways, their operation worked well. Business dealings were restricted, but once a relationship had been established with a FTO official, business could operate on an on-going basis. Opportunities for sales promotion have been in the form of discount deals or perhaps small incentives.

The removal of such a network has created as many headaches as it has new possibilities. All trading is now carried out directly with private companies, of which there are 26,000 with the right to trade with other countries. Many of them have little experience of imports and exports, and a limited command of foreign languages. Another problem is that of credit checking. Under the previous system, Western companies were dealing with the state itself. Now they are at the mercy of local companies which cannot prove that they are creditworthy.

Despite these obstacles, a number of Western companies are involved in export to the East or are in the process of setting up joint ventures. However, once contact has been made, agents found and distribution in place, how do such companies go about marketing their particular products, in a region where the discipline barely exists? In the economies of the West, marketing operates within the framework of supply outweighing demand. In the East, the opposite is true. Many essential foodstuffs are subject to shortages and obtaining luxury items is almost impossible. Marketing, as we know it, is severely limited. Eastern European countries are used to a long tradition of buying whatever is on the market and have little experience of a competitive supply situation. In the short term, the sheer dearth of consumer goods means that many items will sell without promotion or advertising. In the longer term, however, as competition increases, there will be a greater need to establish product benefits and differentials.

Even though marketing, in the conventional sense of the word, may be unheard of, a number of Western companies have seized upon the public relations benefits of marketing by appealing to the aspirations of the consumables-starved Eastern Europeans. Pepsi and Coca-Cola are known almost universally across Eastern Europe and have been tried by significant numbers. Other known names include Nescafé, Nestlé, Levis, Maggi/Knorr, Johnnie Walker and McDonalds. Few have tried these products, but there is a great eagerness among the Eastern Europeans to sample Western goods. When McDonalds opened its first outlet in Moscow in 1990, crowds of people queued up in the street. Traffic-building exercises, which would be a typical technique in the West, were not required.

In the foreseeable future, the most likely use of sales promotion is as a way of educating a target market. Sales promotion, in its typical guise of competitions, premiums and couponing, will not usually be necessary for some time yet. However, sales support information and training material do have an immediate application. The office equipment supplier, Rank Xerox, has devised such a programme.

RANK XEROX

The office equipment market has undergone great expansion in the last two years in Eastern Europe. Major companies such as Minolta, Canon, Ricoh and Toshiba have all branched out into the market, and Rank Xerox has now become one of the key players. A dealer network of 110 contacts throughout Eastern Europe has been set up and it has three offices in the Soviet Union and its first Copy Shop in Poland. A further 20 Copy Shops are planned for the East. Sales support programmes are run to educate dealers and special price deals, such as 13 for the price of 12, are also offered. The biggest proportion of its marketing spend goes on promoting the dealer network, and on education and training. The remainder of the budget goes on attending trade and business fairs; editing brochures in local languages; the supply of promotional items such as T-shirts, bags, lighters and watches; sponsorship activity such as the Romanian Rugby Federation and Czechoslovakian football. Above-the-line advertising is only used to recruit dealers, not to advertise services.

DHL

Courier company DHL, which claims to dominate the Eastern European market with a 65 per cent market share, employs 250 people in Hungary, Poland, Bulgaria and the CIS. Around half of its marketing budget goes on advertising – in newspapers, on television and on billboards. It also uses promotional items such as pens and lighters. Lighters are particularly effective in countries where so many adults are smokers.

Charity fundraising and sponsorship are also being considered.

PIZZA HUT

Sales promotion applications are not just confined to educating the business-to-business customer. The average Muscovite in the street has also been the target of a sales promotion campaign, launched to mark the opening of Russia's first Pizza Hut.

Pizza Hut was set up as a joint venture with Moscow City Council. Resources from all over the world were brought in to train staff to the same standard as other outlets throughout the world. The marketing programme started early. Hoardings around the site and local press advertising informed Muscovites about the restaurant long before the opening.

A launch programme was put together by sales promotion company IMP, which devised a campaign that was very different from any Western European equivalent. Traditionally, Pizza Hut has used trial, traffic and awareness-building for the launch of new restaurants, usually against a background of tough competition and, currently, declining disposable income. In Moscow, the only competition is McDonalds, which regularly has two-and-a-half-hour queues for a Big Mac. Some fundamental problems came to light. Consumers did not know what a pizza was, what they should do with it, how they should eat it, let alone how to use the salad bar!

Leaflets were therefore distributed externally and in-store to help customers. Large queues also enabled staff to hand out information to those waiting. Information on different types, guidance on size and details on starters were featured in the leaflets, which also stressed Pizza Hut's American heritage. Tent cards and place mats continued the education process – customers were guided around the restaurant.

One of the most difficult challenges was how to encourage a high level of spend, but at the same time ensure that table turn was maintained. There was initial concern that people drinking coffee could spend the whole afternoon there, but a gentle reminder that there was a long queue alleviated this.

Pepsi-Cola International recognized that the stores were unlikely to yield retail profit for some time, because all profits have to be reinvested in Moscow. The real benefit was the effect on global brand positioning and, in Western Europe, promotional activity associated with the event.

CONCLUSION

In a region which is evolving and transforming on a day-by-day basis, any plans to tap these more liberal markets must be flexible and exist primarily as an 'extra string' to a company's existing activities. When McDonalds first opened in Moscow, it set up a plan capable of servicing a number of restaurants. Experts from all over Europe were brought in to cater for the upsurge in demand. The project has now been put on hold because of the instability of the country. The Moscow restaurant is still open, but plans for further outlets are on ice. It is unlikely that McDonalds will pack up and go home. In the words of its marketing director Michael Hayden: 'We have poured in too much time and effort – I'm sure it will come right in the end.'

The future potential of the Eastern Europe market should not be ignored, despite its current gloomy situation. When the demand comes, whenever that may be, it could well be monumental. As Lech Walesa has put it: 'British industry would need to work flat out for 20 years to fulfil Poland's consumer needs.'

Eastern European consumers would be only too willing to respond to the subtleties of sales promotion and advertising, but their exposure to both disciplines is limited and will continue to be so until the mid 1990s, when an upturn in consumer demand is expected. The desires and aspirations are already there: across all countries a car made in the West is the item people would most like to own, and videorecorders and automatic washing machines also score highly. People want consumer goods of every conceivable variety. Once competitive supply situations arise there is certain to be an eager response to everything sales promotion offers: premiums; prizes; a chance to obtain goodies at lower cost.

PROPOSED OUTLINE OF EUROPEAN REGULATIONS FOR SALES PROMOTION

INTRODUCTION

What follows is based very closely on the voluntary code of the European Federation of Sales Promotion (EFSP), first adopted in 1992. This EFSP work, however, was intended only to supplement existing national codes of conduct and to be subservient to the many different laws regulating sales promotion in individual countries.

The following regulations, on the contrary, are designed to *replace* and supersede all such existing national laws, regulations and codes, becoming the basis for any European law it may be considered necessary to enact.

PROMOTIONAL ACTIVITIES

The activities relate for the most part to promotions subject to a time limit and having as their general aim an increase in sales, directed at consumers, distribution networks or sales forces.

The activities are based on the principle of awarding additional benefits in the form of such promotion tactics as: premium offers; reduced price and free offers; the distribution of vouchers, coupons and samples; personality promotions; charity-linked promotions; editorial promotions; and prize promotions.

The benefit may, in some cases, not be awarded directly in favour of the consumer, but in favour of an important cause or a fund supported by the consumer and/or by the promoter. They may also relate to promotional activities or services of a long-term nature: consumer clubs; benefits related to after-sales service.

PRINCIPAL DEFINITIONS

Here are a few basic terms used throughout these regulations for which a definition should be provided.

- 'The promoter' – The company promoting its goods or services.
- 'The beneficiary' – Any person or group of people at whom the promotion is directed, be it a private person, an associate, a firm or legal entity.
- 'The intermediaries' – Any person or body, other than the promoter, instructed to implement any form of promotional activity: promotion or publicity advisory agencies, companies specializing in the administration of promotional operations etc.
- 'The product' – The goods or services being promoted.
- 'The benefit' – All products, services, material or financial benefits the beneficiaries receive or may receive in connection with their participation in the promotions.
- 'The media and communication networks' – Any means used to make the beneficiaries aware of the existence of promotions and how to participate. These may be:
  - advertising media, ie billboards, cinema, press, radio, television;
  - direct communication networks, ie mailing networks, telephone, telex and fax etc;
  - advertising material at point of sale, catalogues etc;
  - product packaging, labels on products etc.

BASIC PRINCIPLES

The following basic principles apply to all promotional activity.

LEGALITY

All promotional activity must be legal. It must scrupulously observe all laws which, while not specifically directed at sales promotion, will none the less affect their form, presentation and implementation, eg laws regarding obscenity, blasphemy, race relations, sex discrimination, advertising etc.

RESPECT FOR THE BENEFICIARY

All promotional activity must respect the beneficiary. The promoter or his agents must neither abuse the trust of the participants nor exploit their lack of experience or knowledge.

FAIRNESS

Conditions for participating in and the performance of the promotional activity must be fair for all those concerned.

PUBLIC INTEREST

The planning and performance of any promotional activity must be such that it avoids any conflict with public interest. The promotional activity should not, in particular, entail anything likely to cause or be seen to tolerate violent or anti-social behaviour, material damage or any other damage or injury.

PRESENTATION

Promotions must be presented clearly and honestly so as not to deceive those at whom they are directed or those likely to receive information about them. Whilst it is accepted that promotions will often be presented in a spectacular manner, this presentation must not cause deception in terms of the way it is worded or visualized.

This principle applies to all media or support networks, whatever the nature of the promotional activity involved.

RESTRICTIONS

All factors likely to influence a beneficiary's decision on whether or not to participate in a promotion shall be presented in such a way as to ensure that he is, before becoming involved, aware of any purchase necessary for participation.

HANDLING

Promotions shall be administered quickly and efficiently in order to avoid any justified complaint on the part of the participants.

GENERAL PROVISIONS

1. PROTECTION OF PRIVATE LIVES

a) Promotional activity must respect the private life of the consumer and must therefore be devised and undertaken in such a way that it always leaves the consumer free to decide whether or not to take up the offer.

b) Solicitation of participants for publicity purposes or public relations, related or otherwise to the promotional activity, must be brought to the knowledge of the beneficiary in an unequivocal manner prior to any participation on his part. Permission must, in particular, be obtained from winners to use their names and addresses for any publicity purposes.

c) In the event that data files are used, attempts should be made to verify that the information contained in these files is as accurate as possible.

Moreover, if a consumer requests that his name and address be removed from any file, all steps must be taken to meet this request.

d) Companies using postal or telephone systems and all other intermediaries are reminded that they are responsible for the confidentiality of any file they compile.

2. PROTECTION OF MINORS

a) The term 'minor' means any person under the age of 18.

b) Promotions directed at minors and children in particular must not take advantage of their credulity or their lack of experience. Particular attention should be paid to avoiding any risk of physical, emotional or moral harm.

c) Promotions aimed directly at minors, or likely to attract their attention shall not under any circumstances contain inappropriate benefits or propositions.

d) When a promotional offer awards prizes or other benefits likely to cause conflict between children and their legal representatives (parents or guardians), conditions for participation must clearly include the written approval of the latter.

3. SAFETY

a) All steps must be taken to ensure that safety rules are met. There must in particular be no risk or danger for the beneficiary in receiving promotional products or services offered as a benefit.

b) Precautions must be taken when the promotions are directed at children or when products offered as a benefit for adults are likely to fall into the hands of children.

c) Information and instructions for products offered as a benefit must draw full attention to any dangers each time such dangers may arise.

4. PRESENTATION

a) A promotion must be presented and advertised in such a way that it does not deceive the beneficiary.

b) Whatever the media used, all items of information must meet the provisions of these regulations. The description of promotional offers must not in particular be deceptive as to quality, value, usage or availability, particularly where beneficiaries are not in a position to examine them before they are received.

c) Some operations may involve the assistance of various media (for example, publicity at the point of sale or relayed by radio and TV message). In this case it is necessary to ascertain that the message is likely to be accepted by all the media concerned. Some, notably television, may in fact lay down specific requirements.

d) Everything shall be done within the control of the promoter to ensure that no product announcing any promotion is distributed after the said promotion has ended.

e) The fact that products or services offered as benefits as part of promotional activity may be obtained free of charge does not mean that the duty to give a proper description can be waived.

5. QUALITY OF THE PRODUCTS OR SERVICES OFFERED AS A BENEFIT

Products or services offered as a benefit as part of promotional activity must meet current legislation as regards safety, conditions of use, performance and useful life. Where appropriate, information such as guarantee conditions or after-sales service must be clearly explained.

6. SUITABILITY OF PROMOTIONAL PRODUCTS FOR THEIR TARGET

a) Promotional benefits must not risk offending certain members and/ or segments of the public.

b) Where samples are distributed free of charge to minors or particularly susceptible people, it is necessary to ensure that these samples cannot harm them.

7. TERMINOLOGY USED IN PROMOTIONS

a) Terminology must be clear, complete and easy for the beneficiary to understand.

b) The following information must be clearly explained:

- how to take advantage of the promotional offer or how to receive the goods, services, benefits or refunds arising from the offer;
- where appropriate, the nature and number of proofs of purchase that are required;
- how to participate, including, where appropriate, how to pay and the amount of any carriage or dispatch costs;
- the name and address of the party offering the promotion – where this information is entered on a reply coupon, it shall appear on the part of the document retained by the participant.

8. PARTICIPATION CONDITIONS

a) Restrictions on participation in any promotion must be clearly indicated, particularly the exclusion of any consumers not entitled to benefit from the offer.

b) Where proof of purchase is required as a condition for participation, such a condition must be announced in an unequivocal manner such that the beneficiary is advised of the fact before making his purchase. In particular, all promotion material such as wrappings, labels or packaging must indicate whether or not participation in the promotion is subject to any purchase requirement. This information must be clearly visible to the beneficiary before he makes his purchase.

c) The following two items of information must be shown systematically:

- the date the offer ends or closure date of the promotion;
- where appropriate, any request for additional proof of purchase.

d) where appropriate, the following restrictions shall also be mentioned:

- geographical limits;
- limit in the number of times participation is permitted;
- limit in the number of promotional products or prizes an individual or a household may claim;
- restrictions for a specific period due to prior gain;
- any authorization required, for example, that of parents in the case of a minor.

e) To help intermediaries check promotional stocks and rotation of products involved in a promotional offer, the following information must be clearly entered on external packaging:

- geographical restrictions;

- closure date of operation;
- any duty to stock other goods related to the promotion.

9. AVAILABILITY OF PROMOTIONAL PRODUCTS

a) Entries such as 'for as long as stocks last' do not constitute any dispensation from taking all steps necessary to enable the customer to benefit from the promotional offer.

b) In the event that receipt of the promotional benefit is linked to disbursement or provision of proof of purchase, it is necessary to be able to show that availability assumptions have been the subject of a serious study and that the number of promotional products available is sufficient to meet demand.

c) Where volume and/or time limits are intentionally set on the promotional offer, these limits must be clearly announced to the beneficiary before he becomes involved, and the media involved in communicating the offer must not exaggerate the chances of receiving the benefit or the promotional product.

d) In the event that exceptional, unforeseen demand means that it is impossible to honour the promotional offer, unsuccessful partici- pants shall receive another item of equivalent or higher value. Such intention must be made clear to the participant prior to any involvement on his part. The notion of 'equivalent value' shall be evaluated in terms of the participant's perception of quality, price or cost. Moreover, where stocks are exhausted or delays (beyond the six weeks specified in 10 b, below) arise in meeting demand, all publicity for the offer shall be halted and all applicants shall be informed in writing of the reasons for the delays and the expected date of late delivery.

10. ADMINISTRATION

a) Promotions shall be administered with adequate control facilities and procedures. All precautions possible shall be taken to ensure that the beneficiary has no well-founded reason for complaint.

b) Except in cases where the nature of the products or services on offer make it impossible, applications shall be honoured within six weeks of their receipt. The maximum delivery period shall appear on all promotion material transmitting offer terms.

c) Damaged and defective goods or those that have gone astray due to liability on the part of the sender must be replaced or refunded as quickly as possible, all costs being borne in principle by the sender.

SPECIFIC APPLICATIONS

1. FREE OFFERS

a) The only costs that a consumer may be required to contribute towards an offer which is described as 'free' or 'no purchase required' are the actual costs incurred in applying for or handling the offer, eg telephone, postage.

b) In no case shall the promoter use any of the following means to reduce the cost to him of a free offer:

- changes in the composition or quality or an increase in the price of a product whose purchase gives access to the offer;
- a greater charge than actual costs for handling, transport, postage etc.

c) Care has to be taken in the use of the term 'prize' in order to avoid raising expectations that may not be satisfied. In particular, goods or other benefits for which the majority of prospective participants qualify should not be described as prizes.

d) Trial goods may not be described as 'free' if the beneficiary is asked to bear the cost of returning them, unless any information to the contrary is clearly indicated at the time the offer is announced.

e) Where an offer appears on a product and benefiting from the offer requires several purchases of the product, the need to make additional purchases must be clearly indicated.

f) Where an offer covers two or more items, of which only one is free of charge, it is necessary to ensure that the beneficiary can easily distinguish the free item from those for which payment must be made.

g) Where samples, small items or gifts without obligation to buy are distributed unsolicited through a promotion, it is necessary to ensure that the beneficiary knows that he is under no obligation to buy, that his acceptance does not commit him in any way and that he is not bound to return them.

2. PROMOTIONS IN WHICH PRIZES ARE AWARDED: GAMES OF CHANCE, LOTTERIES, COMPETITIONS

I PARTICIPATION CONDITIONS

Participation procedures must be governed by a clearly drawn-up set of rules so that potential participants do not at any time risk being deceived by the offer made to them. The rules must be easily accessible to any interested party.

The rules shall set out in particular:

- the closing date;
- any age, eligibility requirements;
- any geographical restrictions;
- any restrictions on number of entries or prizes awarded;
- a description of the prizes and any duties or obligations on the part of the winners;
- procedures relating to publication of results;
- use of intellectual and artistic property rights on replies and documents of participants;
- any possibility of exchanging prizes for cash;
- authorization of a parent, guardian etc.

Procedures for obtaining the rules must appear as far as is practically possible on all written forms of communication.

As far as possible, it is recommended that an extract from the rules appear on the various promotion presentation media. This shall include conditions for participation and principal restrictions.

II PUBLICATION OF RESULTS

a) Participants in any promotion in which prizes are awarded must be informed of the date and manner in which the results will be published.

b) The list of big winners, including at least their names and 'region', must be available on request, or published. Such publication must not give rise to costs out of proportion to the cost of the promotion and may not be prejudicial to the interests and private lives of the winners or other participants. One should not forget the risk of harassment that might arise if the information published is sufficiently detailed to enable a third party to locate a winner.

c) Participants in any promotion requiring the sending in of documents arising from personal research or work must be advised of the possibility or otherwise of recovering these documents after the operation has ended.

d) Replies or documents submitted by big winners shall only be published and/or used if such action is in no way contrary to their legitimate interests. Assuming that this is not the case, the method of use shall be clearly set out at the start of the operation and shall appear in the rules.

III PUBLICITY FOR PROMOTIONS IN WHICH PRIZES ARE AWARDED

a) Publicity for promotions in which prizes are to be won shall respect the following provisions:

- the message giving information on the prizes to be won shall specify the nature and number of the main prizes;
- notice of the total amount of the prizes alone shall only be authorized if it is supplemented by a message that meets the requirements set out in the paragraph above;
- the prizes shall be presented in such a way that there can be no confusion in the minds of the participants as to value;
- the prizes shall be presented in the order of their commercial value.

b) The closure date of any promotion shall be clearly specified in every advertisement, on every entry form and on the outside of all packs, packaging or labels. Once announced this date may not be changed except in the event of absolute necessity. An insufficient number of participants or the mediocre quality of entries does not constitute sufficient reason to extend a promotion or refuse distribution of prizes unless this is expressly stipulated at the start of the operation.

c) Expectation of winning a prize shall not be exaggerated and no suggestion of certainty of winning shall be given for as long as winning is not certain.

d) Where a gift or free benefit is granted to all participants over and above the prizes on offer, the distinction between such gifts and prizes to be won must clearly be defined in all promotional material where practically possible.

IV ADMINISTRATION OF PROMOTIONS IN WHICH PRIZES ARE AWARDED

a) A sufficient period of time must be provided for the performance of each stage of a promotion: announcement through distribution, availability of products or services, collection of proofs of purchase, the jury's decision, where appropriate and publication of the results.

b) Where promotions in which prizes are awarded are the subject of a publicity campaign, it is necessary to ensure that the entry forms and products or services necessary for participation are widely available: for example, proof of purchase specific to the promotion.

c) Prizes shall be sent to winners within a maximum period of six weeks from the date of closure of the operation, unless otherwise specified in the rules.

d) Where an element of subjective appraisal is involved in selecting winners in a competition open to the general public, the competition shall be judged either by a person not connected with the organizers or by a jury comprising at least three people not connected with the organizers. In the event of selection at various stages (pre-selection and final selection) the rules shall specify the procedures for each of the stages.

3) PROMOTIONS BENEFITING NON-PROFIT MAKING ORGANIZATIONS OR CAUSES OF PUBLIC INTEREST

These promotions must satisfy the following conditions:

a) where the beneficiary of a promotional activity is a non-profit making organization, the beneficiary must be specified together with its aims;
b) the extent and nature of the advantage to be gained by the charity or good cause should be clearly defined;
c) contributions to the cause made by purchase of a product or products on promotion shall not be overstated;
d) any limit on the contribution made to the beneficiary of the promotion must be clearly specified;
e) particular attention should be paid to promotions of this kind that may involve minors;
f) the promoter must be able to justify the benefit the promotion awards the cause in question.

CONSUMER COMPLAINTS

Consumer complaints about any promotional activity must receive a reply as soon as possible.

Where the complaint requires an investigation of its circumstances it should be acknowledged immediately, with an estimate of the time required to complete the investigation and to report further on its findings.

All replies to complaints which claim an infringement of any of the clauses of these regulations must be accompanied by the address of the authority responsible for the regulations' enforcement.

POPULATIONS AND CURRENCY VALUES

(Note: The following *very* approximate figures are designed only to help the reader understand the relative scale of numbers and costs quoted in the case studies.)

	Approx-imate popula-tion 1990 (millions)	Currency	£1 sterling equals very approx	US$1 equals very approx
Austria	7.7	schilling	20.1	11.6
Belgium	9.9	Belgian franc	59.0	34.0
Denmark	5.1	Danish krone	11.1	6.4
Finland	4.9	markka	7.7	4.4
France	56.5	French franc	9.7	5.6
Germany	63.1	mark	2.9	1.7
Greece	10.1	drachma	333.0	192.0
Ireland	3.5	punt	1.1	0.6
Italy	57.6	lira	2150.0	1245.0
Luxembourg	0.4	Luxembourg franc	59.0	34.0
Netherlands	14.9	guilder	3.2	1.9
Norway	4.2	Norwegian krone	11.2	6.5
Portugal	10.4	escudo	246.0	142.4
Spain	39.0	peseta	180.5	104.5
Sweden	8.6	Swedish krona	10.4	6.0
Switzerland	6.8	Swiss franc	2.6	1.5
UK	57.5	pound	1.0	0.6

INDEX